—————————— THE ——————————

PROMISE

OF THE

Atonement

THE

PROMISE

OF THE

Atonement

CURE FOR BROKEN DREAMS

ESTER RASBAND

CFI
SPRINGVILLE, UTAH

ISBN: 1-55517-795-6
v.1

Published Cedar Fort, Inc.
925 N. Main Springville, UT, 84663
www.cedarfort.com

Distributed by:

Cover design by Nicole Williams
Cover design © 2005 by Lyle Mortimer

Printed in the United States of America
10 9 8 7 6 5 4 3 2 1

Printed on acid-free paper

Great peace have they which love thy law:
and nothing shall offend them.

—Psalm 119:165

DEDICATION

To Jim, of course.

CONTENTS

ACKNOWLEDGMENTS

Gratitude takes up such a small portion of the space in a book, and yet it responds to content and support that loom large in the book's creation.

My greatest thanks, of course, goes to those whose stories I tell. It is not easy for folks to have their suffering exposed. To air the pain of those who confided in me as I delved into this subject was something I did with reluctance but with a desire to teach a concept. I tried hard not to exploit their hurt by using their agony to enhance my writing. If I have added to anyone's pain, I beg forgiveness. I pray, instead, that my testimony will give them added strength.

To my friends who read either all or part of the manuscript and who offered suggestions and criticism, I give my thanks. To those who engaged in discussion of the ideas in the book, I want you to know that your stimulus was indispensable. Debate and conversation are the lifeblood of my work.

I would also like to thank Leslie Stitt, who was a valued and objective editor. Colleen Stohlton made a suggestion that spawned a new first chapter. My two daughters-in-law, Kelley and Mary Rasband, tirelessly read and reread the manuscript, and both made suggestions that either clarified or expanded my message. My two sons, Jim and Win Rasband, also made a difference in the book, particularly in the area of debate and discussion of ideas. Their excitement about my thesis was a great asset.

Thanks also to the people at Cedar Fort, who saw and shared my vision.

Finally, and most of all, I want to thank my husband, Jim. His encouragement has been important to all of my books, but he can take particular credit for this one. He was the one who said it was "necessary" to write it. He gently goaded me when my "natural man" would have thought it not worth the effort and set it aside. He did most of the research. He critically said, "No, you haven't got it yet; try that chapter again." And he offered encouragement with the words: "Oh, yes. That's it. I really like it."

~ 1 ~

THE CURE FOR BROKEN DREAMS

His age was still in single digits when his father left. He and his dying mother were penniless, and before he could shave he made his way alone. The pain of being abandoned has been pervasive and the hardship has lasted a lifetime.

Her father came to her bed almost every night from the time she was nine years old. Twice she tried to be a wife and failed. She is aged now, bitter and lonely.

Their only daughter was raped and killed by a neighbor. The possible last moments of her life are replayed in their minds over and over again. Years later, productivity and contentment still evade them.

The names of these who are so hurt have not been given here because their name is legion. Mortals are wretchedly wounded by the sins of their fellow beings.

It must have been heartrending for our Father in Heaven

1

to know that allowing agency would result in unbidden horror for some of his children, and a degree of sorrow for all of them. Nevertheless, agency is an essential element of this second estate. Without it there could be no real test and therefore, no opportunity to pass the test. Sadly, the freedom to hurt others is inherent in this necessary state.

But our Father in Heaven is committed to more than just agency. He has an equal commitment to justice—not just the justice that means punishment of a perpetrator but also the justice that means the honoring of "victims' rights." He is pledged to see that victims are able to receive a judgment that guarantees them wholeness and full restitution. That is the justice that makes agency a perfect plan.—perfect not because it is a painless plan (we all know that isn't the case) but because it provides the test without permanent damage.

All damage can be completely overcome by the supreme energy of an infinite atonement. God the Father has in the power of his Son's mercy the miracle of total healing—the miracle of unlimited justice. How that must have comforted him as he placed us here. He could require us to endure to the end because he and his Son were committed to making it possible for there to *be* an end—an end to suffering, an end to hurt, an end to the Fall itself.

The knowledge that the Atonement provides the doorway to complete fairness is a source of peace and quietude. But we need to *understand* justice—to know what fairness means—so that we can rely on that comfort and let it penetrate our souls. If we do not understand it we won't trust in it. We will not be able to forgive or to feel forgiveness, we may retreat from risk and limit the joy in relationships. Without understanding justice, we may be able to endure mortal trial, but we probably will not be able to "endure it well." And having enough trust to rely on divine justice is a challenge for mankind. The pain of being victims overwhelms us. The fear of facing life with our pains can be paralyzing and makes us feel hopeless.

Life feels unfair. In order to feel the fairness of the Lord's justice system, we have to take a leap of faith, but facing that leap, we experience a moment of hesitation. Perhaps the best example of this hesitation comes from our ancient ancestors. The Old Testament seems an unlikely place to turn to for a peaceful understanding of the Atonement—considering our predisposition to think of the Old Testament as harsh—but the blueprint for peace is there. The fear of the ancient Israelites was not really so different from that which all of us feel when we lack understanding. They were simply afraid. They were unable to see the hope and comfort that being in the presence of God would bring.

So God gave to Moses a law that contained the elements of perfect justice so that people could learn what was required for fairness and integrity of the order. Then, with the promise that a loving master would go with them to the judgment and insure that justice would be done, he invited them to embark on a journey toward the understanding that would bring them peace.

Paul told the people of his day that the law of Moses was a schoolmaster that would bring them to Christ, and it is still that.

Those who, even today, experience the fear and anguish left by those who hurt them can use the ancient schoolmaster to help them understand and look forward to the justice of the Atonement with its thorough healing and perfect fairness. And once this kind of justice is understood, consolation and reassurance will be found there.

With that help, we can develop a hope that trades our nightmares for sweet rest. With that help we can have that rest on a profound level. Or, as C. S. Lewis said:

"For broken dreams, the cure is dream again, and deeper."[1]

Note

1. *The Quotable Lewis,* ed. Wayne Martindale and Jerry Root (Wheaton, Ill.: Tyndale House Publishers, 1989), 167.

~ 2 ~

VICTIMS' RIGHTS LAW

An old story (I don't know if it's fiction or fact) tells of a banquet given to honor Christopher Columbus when he returned to Europe after his earth-expanding voyage.

In addition to those who were there to praise him, there were some detractors who declared that all he did was get in a boat and sail west. "Easy enough," they said, "that any fool could do it." Columbus picked up a hard-boiled egg from the banquet table and asked the detractors to stand it on end. All tried but no one succeeded. Columbus picked up the egg and rapped it on the table, breaking the shell on one end and creating a self-platform on which the egg did indeed stand on end.

"Easy enough," he said, "that any fool could do it." Then, after a pause, he added, "Once someone shows you how."

I think of that story every now and again when someone gives me an insight into the gospel—when a principle that I had thought difficult or a concept that I had not understood suddenly becomes plain and precious. Sometimes—with the insight of the gospel—the truth is so obvious that I can almost hear the voice of Columbus: "Easy enough that any fool could know it . . . once someone shows you how."

I had such an experience one evening regarding a common misunderstanding relating to the Atonement—a misconception that creates a barrier to peace in those who have been hurt by others. It is the mistaken notion that we are required to excuse those who have trespassed against us, and that we must discount the pain they have caused us.

One night that view was rapped on the table and stood on end, as it were, and I began to feel peace from knowing that justice will not be forfeited and will be given full weight. This happened one evening when my husband made the short trip from his study into mine, bringing the book he was reading. He sat down and asked if I had a minute. I turned in my chair and he began:

"I've been intrigued that the justice system of the law of Moses is referred to as 'Victim's Rights Law.' What do you think about that?"

"Fascinating," I answered. From that one statement all my understanding and feelings about the Atonement suddenly came together. A concept had been rapped on end for me. It seemed simple because someone had shown me how.

"If that's an accurate definition of the law of Moses, then the Atonement had to honor and fulfill 'victim's rights.' Christ said that he'd fulfill every jot and tittle of the Law, so if victim's rights are what the law of Moses is about, then victims have rights, and the Atonement has to satisfy them. That means that the Atonement would have to make victims whole."

We were both quiet for a moment. "We always think about the Atonement making *sinners* whole, but that would be an emphasis on the *sinned against*."

"Yes," my husband was pensive for a moment. "But isn't accepting the Atonement all about forgiving and relinquishing any . . ." and he paused a moment as he thought about the inference, "any victims' rights."

"Is it?" I asked him. "Is it really? Certainly accepting the Atonement is all about forgiving, but is relinquishing the same as forgiving? Maybe forgiving means something other than what we've always thought."

"Yes, maybe so," my husband said slowly. "If the law of Moses is what the Atonement fulfills, then I guess it would have a lot of answers about what forgiveness means, and about what rights victims have, and a lot more about the Atonement. I guess we don't give the law of Moses enough attention."

He was right. We don't. But for us, that state of mind was about to change.

We were about to learn what C. S. Lewis meant when he said: "To forgive does *not* mean to excuse."[1] We were about to recognize the peace that comes from having our suffering given full undiscounted weight. We were about to know that those who have been damaged by the sins of others will be mercifully and miraculously healed.

We had previously tended to focus on the Atonement's benefit to the sinner instead of to the one sinned against. We had failed to realize that Christ is the Savior of the sinner precisely because he stands ready to make restitution by paying the debt that the sinner owes to him whom he has sinned against. The debt will be paid with thorough healing. This fact is made clear by the law of Moses. Understanding that fact gives comfort to both victim and victimizer. Forgiving and being forgiven are therefore linked in reality, not just in requirement. Both are a matter of accepting Christ as the payer of the debt.

Acceptance of the Atonement is not, and never could be, a rejection of justice. It is the assurance of it.

The Lord gave a law to Moses that, because it deals so thoroughly with justice, teaches us about mercy as well. Paul, as it turns out, gave us a major clue to understanding mercy itself when he reminded us that the law of Moses is a schoolmaster that can bring us to Christ. But I get ahead of myself.

Note

1. C. S. Lewis, *The Weight of Glory*, ed. Walter Hooper (New York: Simon & Schuster, Touchstone Books, 1996), 133.

~ 3 ~

"The Demands of Justice"

The Law that the Lord gave to Moses is neither archaic nor irrelevant—its reputation notwithstanding. In truth, the issues of the Law are ageless and the relevance fairly bristles. Still, detail can be difficult and is required to understand the demands of justice as they are presented in the Law. So bear with me, please, as we take a rather lengthy look at the law of Moses.

~

We join the children of Israel in the wilderness about three months after they have left Egypt. The diet: manna. The mood: hopeful. They desire to make covenants with the Lord, but they hear his voice as he gives them the Ten Commandments, and they are frightened.[1]

At this point, they turn away from seeking direct contact with God. Clearly the ancient Israelites came face-to- face with their lack of readiness. Unable or unwilling to accept the laws of the higher priesthood with which their preslavery ancestors had been blessed, they wanted something they could do.[2] The Lord responded by giving Moses an extensive code for them to live by, a system of regulations that could prepare them to someday receive the higher law again. When God revealed the portion dealing with interpersonal conduct, he called it *the judgments*.

"Now these are the *judgments* which thou shalt set before them" (Exodus 21:1; emphasis added).

It's a good word that the King James translators have given us here: "judgments" is, to be sure, an accurate rendering of the Hebrew[3] and implies both a deep and a broad meaning of what is to follow. This word suggests not just the commands, but the resulting accountability those commands bring with them. Here are the consequences that attach. Here's the Law and the resulting responsibility under the Law. And the word *judgments* is the word we use to refer to a legal requirement to *meet* that responsibility. The very word sets up the accountability as a *debt*. *Judgments* is a powerful word, and the use of it—all by itself—lends authority to what is to follow.

"Now these are the judgments which thou shalt set before them."

It is particularly fascinating to consider how the judgments begin. The very first set of rules in the law of Moses details the requirements of the master-servant relationship (Exodus 21:2–11). It might be considered odd to describe the conduct expected of masters and servants first, until we remember how often the Lord and his prophets refer to the Lord as *master* and to us as his *servants*. The judgments described here are certainly a type for becoming a permanently bonded servant of the Lord.

> And if the servant shall plainly say, I love my master, my wife, and my children; I will not go out free: Then *his master* shall bring him unto *the judges*; he shall also bring him to the door, or unto the doorpost; and . . . he shall serve [his master] for ever. (Exodus 21:5–6; emphasis added)

These rules of the master-servant relationship seem intended to remind the children of Israel—as the prophet Abinadi did so many centuries later—that the law of Moses was meant "to keep them in remembrance of God and their duty towards him"

(Mosiah 13:30). These master-servant rules promise that the Savior will pay the judgments due both from us and to us if we achieve the love necessary to be counted as his servants forever. That is what will happen when he takes us "to the judges."[4] Clearly, as servants of a divine master, we are to love him and our families if we want to be his servants forever and want him to assume the responsibility for us as both debtors and victims. If we choose to read these verses as applicable to only mortal masters and servants we are sorely disadvantaged in understanding the many important applications of the Law.

Directly following this beginning—second only to clarifying our relationship to our master—come those sections that apply to those who wrong another or who are wronged by another. This is the "demands of justice" part: the part where those who have been wronged by others can find patience and hope. We'll speak of those "requirements of the Law" in terms of "ground rules."

The first ground rule—placed first for us by sheer volume of verses—is the assertion that healing the victim is paramount. When someone has been wronged, he must be made whole. This can be, and generally is, called "victims' rights law." By this label we accurately summarize the justice system of the law of Moses.

Speaking of the perpetrator, the Lord says: "He shall pay for the loss of [the victim's] time, and shall cause [the victim] to be thoroughly healed" (Exodus 21: 19).

And again: "for he should make full restitution; if he have nothing, then he shall be sold for his theft" (Exodus 22: 3).

And again: "If a man shall cause a field or vineyard to be eaten . . . of the best of his own field; and of the best of his own vineyard, shall he make restitution. If fire break out . . . he that kindled the fire shall surely make restitution" (Exodus 22: 5–6).

And so on.

It is quickly clear that the law of Moses makes the victim's restitution all-important and that making that restitution is the responsibility of the victimizer. In all cases, the premier goal is that the victim be made whole—even if it means that the victimizer must be sold into servitude to pay the debt.

The second ground rule is that restitution can take many forms. I've already quoted verses where fruit of the field is restitution. Labor for the victim can also make the payment. Money payments can redeem the perpetrator from his debt to his victim in some cases. Or perhaps, as already mentioned, the perpetrator can be sold into servitude for payment toward making the victim whole again. The important thing to remember here is that restitution is the goal and that victimizers are required to be committed to that goal.

A truth that will not escape those who suffer, of course, is that for many offenses, a victimizer *cannot* fully restore his victim—not in any form of payment. The damage is just too profound. No matter the method or the intensity with which the restoration effort is made, the repentant debtor is sure to feel his own inadequacy in this regard—an inadequacy that is also keenly felt by his victim. But remember those early verses about having our master go with us to the judges when we fully express our love for him. The form of payment from the master can and will be miraculous and omnipotent. As the perpetrator makes the required effort of the law, he should see both the importance of restitution *and* the fact that the miracle of complete wholeness can come only from God. As a debtor gives his whole effort to finding a way to make the payment, he becomes more aware of his inadequacies and he wants his responsibility for the debt absolved by the divine proxy. The alternative, of course, would be to cast about in the agony of his inadequacy forever.

A third ground rule is that restitution has to be made (the victim must be made whole) no matter whether the damage inflicted was purely accidental, caused by negligence, or committed with malice aforethought. The wholeness requirement is all-inclusive.

However, the malice or the negligence makes a difference in determining whether restitution to wholeness is enough. With malice or negligence justice requires that additional damages be paid.[5] The amount of damages paid to a victim is multiplied when cunning or carelessness is proven. I've come to call this the "intent of the heart" ground rule. Clearly our hearts do make a difference.

The fourth "ground rule" is that when restitution is not made, the eye-for-eye punishment of the *lex talion* must follow. *Lex talion* is Latin for "the law of retaliation" and is the term scholars use for the "eye-for-an-eye" principle of the law of Moses. The eye-for-an-eye principle is expressed in Exodus where the Lord first speaks of the need for punishment. There, the Lord directs that the *lex talion* is triggered "if any mischief follow" the initial wrong visited upon another (Exodus 21: 23–26). This reference to "mischief" that can follow the initial wrong does not refer to an independent wrong but to a compounding of the initial one. Thus, when we hurt another and then try to escape responsibility for so doing, that would be mischief. Where a perpetrator tries to hide, or to give less than full restitution by weighting the scales or by claiming he hasn't the means, that would be mischief. If one begrudges the debt of restitution—gives sloppy work or obstructive performance—that would be mischief. Mischief, in other words, is what results when damage is not recompensed and injury is therefore continued or compounded.[6] For that reason, I have come to call the dramatic punishments that the Mosaic law sets out: The Mischief Consequence.

But the *lex talion*[7] is more than just a limitation on the punishment. It is a symbol of the fact that the equivalency must be given to a victim. I think of the mischief consequence of having a poetic nature—seeing that it is a profound symbol of restitution. The symbolic nature of an eye for an eye fills me with awe for the Lord's way. The symbol emphasizes what the victim suffered, and it is designed to fit the crime. An eye for an eye turns out to be, at its very core, an emblem of *thwarted* restitution.

The fifth ground rule presents itself in a much more subtle way. The victim has the responsibility to seek a judgment for restitution (or the alternative punishment). The verses of the Law do not present a prosecutorial bureaucracy, and the victim is the person who would take his victimizer and the required witnesses "to the judges."

As a matter of practice, Israelites did indeed live their version of the law with that individual responsibility. Victims took the complaints and witnesses to the judge or judges. Later the Israelites took their evidence and their witnesses to the gates of the city, where the elders of Israel rendered a judgment. It appears that damages were not awarded to the injured party without effort from the injured party.

This too is laden with atonement portending. Those who desire the Lord's atoning sacrifice for their suffering have a responsibility to seek that comfort. They must go to the judges, and the ultimate victim—the Savior—has promised that when they bond themselves to him forever he will go to the judges with them.

A sixth ground rule: Mercy is an important principle. Probably because of the way the Law was later interpreted by the scribes and Pharisees, many do not identify this as part of the law of Moses. But it is clearly there.

"If thou at all take thy neighbor's raiment to pledge, thou shalt deliver it unto him by that the sun goeth down: For that is his covering only, it is his raiment for his skin: wherein shall he sleep? And it shall come to pass, when he crieth unto me, that I will hear; for I am gracious" (Exodus 22:26–27).

In other words, if a man has victimized you and must pay you the debt that victimization requires, and if that man has only his coat with which to pay the debt and so he does give you his coat in payment, then the poor man will be cold when night comes. Don't leave him cold in the night. Return his coat. And in future time, when the poor cold debtor cries out to the Lord, the Lord also will give him grace—or mercy.

And again: "If thou see the ass of him that hateth thee lying under his burden, and wouldst forbear to help him, thou shalt surely help with him" (Exodus 23:5).

In other words, your neighbor's hatred of you should not stop you from doing the right thing—from relieving suffering where relief is needed—even for an enemy. Mercy is important. While the victim is quite literally entitled to eye for eye, tooth for tooth, hand for hand, arm for arm—the law of Moses was *never* intended to make it okay for a victim to give hate for hate. Paul's words to the Romans so many centuries later state one of those principles that has never changed:

"Recompense to no man evil for evil" (Romans 12:17). Reading these sections of the Law makes it obvious that the God of the Old Testament is the same as the God of the New. What's more, he sets up in these verses a preparation for receiving grace on the condition of crying unto him. The call for mercy and its promise of it from the Lord on condition of crying unto him does serve to give a more complete foreshadow as to what would be available in the atoning sacrifice of Jesus Christ. This "mercy is important" ground rule may be the most significant of all in creating a type to bring the children of Israel to Christ.

"And for this intent we keep the law of Moses, it pointing our souls to [Christ]; and for this cause it is sanctified unto us for righteousness" (Jacob 4:5).

In summary, these are the ground rules of the judgments.

- Healing of the victim is paramount. Full restitution must be made.

- Restitution can take many forms.

- The malice or negligence makes a difference in determining the amount of damages.
- Punishment must be meted out if restitution is not made.
- The victim is responsible to seek a judgment for restitution.
- Mercy is an important principle.

⌒

Fast-forward, now, to the mortal life of Christ. It is a far different world than the one Moses left at the banks of the River Jordan. The law of Moses is no longer pointing the souls of the Jews to Christ. It was indeed the "schoolmaster to bring [them] unto Christ" (Galatians 3:24). But that isn't the way they received it. I like the way Abinadi describes it:

"And now, did they understand the Law? I say unto you, Nay, they did not all understand the Law: and this because of the hardness of their hearts; for they understood not that there could not any man be saved except it were through the redemption of God" (Mosiah 13:32).

Perhaps they didn't like the idea of being so dependent on a Savior. In any event, they didn't understand the Law and they didn't live it—at least not the way it was intended. Abinadi's words suggest that they, as a people, had *never* understood the Law. Indeed it is hard to find evidence of understanding in their history. We have record of at least once when it was utterly abandoned and forgotten. In the days of King Josiah a high priest was rummaging around in the Temple and rediscovered the Law. Amazed at its very existence, he took the book of the law to the King. Josiah was a righteous leader, who "rent his clothes" at how far his people had strayed from the Law, but he was not really successful in bringing them back to it (2 Kings 22).

After the Babylonian captivity the Jews went to the opposite extreme. It was an equally damning posture. Having suffered the pain of losing the Lord's protection, they made up a lot of rules of their own to help them (as they supposed) live the law. Sadly, they looked well beyond the mark (Jacob 4:14). The simple foundational law that the Lord had given them was distorted to the point of losing its preparatory purpose. The man-made "fences" built around the Law ended up keeping them away from it more than inside of it. To the Pharisees their own rules became an end in themselves instead of the means to an end, which the Lord designed the original law to be. Their "understanding" of the Law—always deficit—now was distorted beyond recognition. Eye for an eye had become the law of retribution. Hate for hate had found its way into their interpretation; mercy was largely forgotten.

With that in mind, go with me up the mountain with the disciples as they went to hear the Savior deliver the Sermon on the Mount. Hear with them—for the first time—the Beatitudes. Meekness and mercy. Peacemaking and submission. In their victims' role (perhaps even in their role as Roman subjects), the Lord's message must have seemed to them—as to many now—to be a contradiction to the laws of justice that they had been given. The Beatitudes wouldn't (at the level of their understanding) seem to offer full restitution or consequences for mischief. As we listen to the Beatitudes with their ears, we need to remember that their society's custom had polluted the law that was initially given and they were products of that society. Besides, even knowing the original judgments would have focused them on victim's rights. It must have sounded to them as if they were being asked to give up that sense of justice. In their world, restitution was antagonistically sought and a hardened, aggressive heart was not looked down upon. Hate for hate was their conditioning. When they heard the words of the meek and humbling Beatitudes, confusion must have overtaken them. I can't imagine otherwise. I can be certain that they shared Mosiah's feelings that the Law was correct because it had been "given them by the hand of the Lord" (Mosiah 29:25). Was this not the very Lord who now addressed them? They must have believed, as Abinadi did, that it was "a law which they were to observe strictly from day to day to keep them in remembrance of God and their duty towards him" (Mosiah 13:31). But the Law had been polluted in their culture, and their understanding of it could not have been as keen as Abinadi's or Mosiah's. And this meekness and mourning, this peacemaking—it wasn't what they understood the Law to be.

Now, here on the mountain, Christ was giving them the higher law. Even though commitment to the Lord was their fondest and most loving desire, they had to be puzzled. They stood there in humility and love, but they must also have been bewildered.

Jesus saw into their eager hearts and willing minds and was moved to reassure them:

"I am not come to destroy, but to fulfill. For verily I say unto you, Till heaven and earth pass, one jot or one tittle shall in no wise pass from the law, till all be fulfilled" (Matthew 5:17–18).

Christ is not talking here of only fulfilling the ritual practices, such as that of blood sacrifice with his own blood, which, of course we know he would surely do. No, considering the content of the Beatitudes, it seems sure here that he is reassuring his disciples regarding more than their ritual only. With the words, "not one jot or one tittle," he is talking about justice as well. Those all-important laws of restitution must also be fulfilled. He was reassuring them about victim's rights.

It was a part of that same sermon when the Lord gave them direction as to how to pray. He said, "Forgive us our debts as we forgive our debtors" (Matthew 6:12). He used an interesting choice of words: "debts" and "debtors." Whom did they owe? What did they owe? Who owed *them* and what was owed? In both Luke and 3 Nephi the Lord expands on that thought and makes it clear that those who *owe* you are those who have trespassed against you, and those *you* owe are those against whom you have trespassed.

"And forgive us our sins; for we also forgive every one that is indebted to us" (Luke 11:4). "For, if ye forgive men their trespasses your heavenly Father will also forgive you" (3 Nephi 13:14).

It seems clear to me that in these verses (as well as in parables and other directives[8]) the Lord is referring to the fact that victims are owed wholeness from their victimizers. That is the Law under which his hearers lived. That is the debt to which he refers. That is the debt that we owe to others and that is the debt that is owed to us. Hurting another incurs a debt, a debt to make that other person whole and healed. The atoning sacrifice is intended to pay that debt for us and to us. Or else it could not fulfill every jot and tittle of the Law.

Justice in the Law means restitution. And the Atonement satisfies the demands of justice. In the words of Amulek, "And behold, this is the whole meaning of the law, every whit pointing to that great and last sacrifice" (Alma 34:14).

Peter referred to the time when Christ would come again as "the times of restitution of all things" (Acts 3:21). Surely it is true that he was referring to the fact that Christ was to bring a restoration of the gospel and the dispensation of the fullness of times.[9] But he was talking to people who had the Old Testament. "Restitution" would have had a legal meaning to them as well.

The principle of restitution pointed to the atoning sacrifice of Christ as surely as the scapegoat or the blood on the doorpost. According to the trustworthy words of the Lawgiver himself, the awarded judgment of restitution is a debt that will be collected. The Law has to be fulfilled. Healing and restoration are a part of the Atonement that Christ has, as his work and glory, a mind to give us. And that fact does indeed determine what it means to forgive and to be forgiven.

Notes

1. Exodus 19:8; 20:18.

2. Exodus 24:3.

3. The Hebrew word here (a noun) comes from the root verb "to judge, to pronounce sentence, to vindicate," or "to punish." The noun is defined as "verdict" and implies "a right" (James Strong, *Hebrew and Chaldee Dictionary of the Old Testament* [Iowa Falls, Iowa: World Bible Publishers, 1986], 98, 159).

4. Note also the temple imagery here.

5. Deuteronomy 19:4–5; Exodus 21:28–29, 33–34; 22:9.

6. The Hebrew word translated here as *mischief* is defined in Benjamin Davidson's *The Analytical Hebrew and Chaldee Lexicon* (Grand Rapids, Mich.: Zondervan Publishing House, 1970, 37) as "hurt" or "injury." Indeed, the Hebrew word in these Exodus 21 verses is a different word than those translated as *mischief* in other Old Testament verses. Nevertheless, I came to relish the King James word because it spoke so well to describe the conditions of the Law as it was lived. The punishment was rare because victimizers more often chose to make restitution. Deuteronomy 17:8–13 talks of one of the specific crimes for which a life for a life is required.

7. It is interesting that the entire concept of the *lex talion* produces so much disagreement among Old Testament scholars. In part, this may be because the Old Testament information on the *lex talion* is rather sketchy. There are only three references, and the emphasis is much more consistently and thoroughly on the law of restitution itself. Many scholars, in fact, believe that the eye-for-an-eye doctrine is not literal at all but simply refers back to the requirement of restitution. Some believe that the *lex talion* is only a symbolic way of expressing that "the punishment must fit the crime."

I did encounter scholars who see the *lex talion* as literally authentic, but they are few. Hans Jochen Boecker, a German scholar, says that he thinks the reason "there are so many misconceptions on this subject" is that the *context* of the *talion* is misunderstood. It "is not in any way a principle for interhuman behaviour; it does not correspond to our modern 'whatever you do to me I shall do to you.' It was valid only as the official sentence of a properly constituted court" (*Law and the Administration of Justice in the Old Testament and Ancient East,* trans. Jeremy Moiser [Minneapolis, Minn.: Augsburg Publishing House, 1980], 175).

Despite a few like Boecker, the vast majority remain loath to believe that the *lex talion* is genuine and that God's law requires such specific justice. This reluctance cannot be explained solely by the fact that references to the *lex talion* in the Old Testament are sketchy. Like so many things that are not understood without seeing them through the eyes of the restored gospel, the necessity for a doctrine of punishment is more easily appreciated in the clear light of modern revelation.

As Alma said, "How could there be a law save there was a punishment? . . . But there is a law given and a punishment affixed, and a repentance granted; which repentance mercy claimeth" (Alma 42:17, 22).

The punishment phase is authentic and literal. LDS scholar Victor Ludlow points out that the punishment functions as a "choice" for the perpetrator. He can either make restitution or suffer in like fashion (*Unlocking the Old Testament* [Salt Lake City: Deseret Book, 1981], 39). This is precisely the choice that the Savior offers us by offering restitution through the Atonement (restitution being impossible for us to make by ourselves).

8. Matthew 18:22 n.

9. This too is a matter of wholeness. Mankind is victim of those who took the plainness of the law from the scriptures—whether it be through ignorance or intent.

~ 4 ~

UNDERSTANDING JUSTICE AND THE DIFFICULTIES OF FORGIVENESS

The great value of understanding justice and its fulfillment was brought forcefully to my mind by a conversation with an inspiring woman who drove me to the airport after a conference. We had been talking about forgiveness as an abstract principle and had both acknowledged how difficult forgiveness can be.

After a few minutes, the conversation was not abstract any more. It became concrete and specific.

"It's my children," she said, honoring me with her confidence. "They've all had a very hard time in life." And she told me a tale of tragedy that wrenched my heart. All of her children had been molested when they were small. The molester was a young man that she and her husband had taken into their home in pure charity. I was stricken with sadness. All I could say was, "Oh no!"

She went on. "The children have suffered with it their whole lives and are still suffering. Every life advance has been painful— some have been impossible." There was a silent moment or two.

Finally I asked her a question: "And the man, where is he now? In prison?"

"No," she said. "That's the worst of it. He's walking around free. He's respected in his community and behaves as if it were nothing. To our family it was *not* nothing. We do not have a day without paying the price for his sin. He's walking around and I guess I'm supposed to say that everything's okay, but everything is not okay. Maybe if I thought he had changed, but I don't think he has."

"Has he ever apologized? Sought your forgiveness?"

"Oh no. If he had, even that might make it easier. But he's totally unrepentant. At least I think I can take as evidence that he is unrepentant the fact that he's never asked our forgiveness. I tell you, it's really hard. And when I hear that not forgiving leaves us as the greater sinner, well, it is just not easy."[1]

The sadness that I felt for this good sister was something I found myself feeling time and time again during the period of research and conversations about forgiveness that preceded this writing. Even when loving children of their Father in Heaven want deeply to obey the commandment to "forgive all men," difficulties loom large. The requirement is most complicated for those who have been severely victimized, but no matter the degree, it turns out that forgiving is hard. I came to know and feel that intensely. Forgiving is hard.

There are three major categories of reasons for the struggle.

We Have to Bear the Burden

This is the sticking point we hear about so often on the evening news. It is mentioned almost every time there is a tragedy where a parent has lost a child or a child has lost a parent. Invariably we hear some form of this: "Well, he says he's sorry, but he's walking around alive and healthy and our child will never be alive again. Nothing that happens to his killer will ever bring back our child." Or "My wife will never see her children grow up. She won't be there to get her little girl ready for a wedding or watch her little boy play baseball. My little children will grow up without a mother."

The offense against us need not be anything so grievous as a lost loved one for us to feel that it is too hard to forgive when we must go on bearing the burden. Each of us lives every day with the pain caused by those we must forgive. It seems a high price to pay for the sin of another. And that makes forgiving hard. This is true whether the offenses are large or small.

A woman whose husband left her now has to use every bit of her energy just to cope with the feelings of rejection. Her desperate need to be loved almost paralyzes her. When she looks in the mirror she sees the despondent image of what-might-have-been and she says that she just can't forgive him for leaving her. The burden she continues to bear is too great.

A young man with hypercritical parents lives every day with his parents' faultfinding ringing in his ears. His confidence suffers and it is not easy to forgive them while he's paying such a high price.

A young woman whose husband brought home the consequence of his infidelity in the form a sexually transmitted disease will be barren and in pain for the rest of her mortal life. The high price is ever present.

A woman who became pregnant and HIV positive as a result of a rape faces bearing a handicapped child and a painful, shortened life. The burden is great.

Two children, orphaned by a drunk driver, suffer feelings of abandonment and difficult adjustment in a strange home. The pain must be profound.

A child who was bullied in the school yard struggles his whole life to overcome feelings of rejection and isolation. His pain too is real and intense.

Whether the suffering is slight or serious, forgiving is hard because people feel that they must continue to pay the price. It isn't fair—they are suffering the consequences of someone else's sinful behavior.

We Can't Discount What We Know Is Wrong

It's hard to forgive because people feel they are being asked to close their eyes to the offenses against them. They feel that they must discount those offenses; that they must pretend the pain doesn't matter.

Our very language encourages us to respond to apology with "it's nothing," or "that's all right." And the English language is not alone here. Other languages invite that same sort of response. No wonder people feel that in order to forgive they have to actually pretend that it's "no problem." We think that's what forgiveness means—that that's what is required of us—to call the offense "nothing."

But it isn't "nothing." It is a problem. We've been *hurt,* and to dismiss it as *de rien* or *de nada* is just too hard. To have to say "No problem" or "It's all right" when we really aren't all right seems not only unfair but also untruthful.

More than once I have heard (and probably you have heard it too): "I can't pretend this never happened. It happened. And you want me to forgive—to say it doesn't matter. It *does* matter!"

C. S. Lewis talks of this mistaken belief. He says:

> Forgiving does not mean excusing. Many people seem to think it does. They think if you ask them to forgive someone who has cheated or bullied them, you are trying to make out that there was really no cheating or no bullying. But if that were so, there would be nothing to forgive.[2]

This misconception—the idea that excusing and discounting is expected of us—does indeed make forgiveness hard.

I wonder if this is one case where the accepted "manners" have failed at leading us to a higher civilization. Wouldn't it be better—more purging for both parties—if instead of "It's nothing," we said, "I forgive you." But that would be charity, wouldn't it?

And charity—scriptural grandeur notwithstanding—has become a dirty word in our society. So, instead we are expected to give a response that makes the offender feel better about himself— something that can create the fantasy that he has never offended. Our society seems to order that politeness requires discounting the damage and (for most of us) *that makes forgiving hard.*

But He Hasn't Asked for Forgiveness!

This third category of difficulty has its root in our natural man's distaste for unilateral action. "I'll forgive him," we hear, "if he *asks* for forgiveness. But he isn't the least bit repentant. He has never apologized." President Spencer W. Kimball acknowledged this particular difficulty: "To forgive one who is mean and offensive is the act of one near to perfect, and especially if the offender is not repentant."[3]

It is not uncommon for members of the Church even to believe that they are justified in refusing forgiveness to the unrepentant. They point to scripture or other instruction that is intended for Priesthood leaders regarding forgiveness. Many of these references do instruct a priesthood leader to require repentance before restoring or maintaining the full fellowship of the Church. But there is a vast difference between the expectation of one representing the Lord as a judge in Israel and one who is the victim of a sinner's sin. As the scriptures say over and over, and particularly plainly in Doctrine and Covenants 64:10: "I, the Lord, will forgive whom I will forgive, but of you it is required to forgive all men."

And that's hard!

Our hearts respond to the uncomforted. The difficulties with forgiveness are real and understandable. It's hard to forgive when we feel we have to live with the damage that has been done to us. It's hard when we can't say inside that it doesn't matter when it obviously does. It's hard because those who have sinned against us are sometimes mean and offensive, and often have not asked for forgiveness. So many people carry such heavy weights. No wonder that the obstacles seem insurmountable.

I think of the good sister with whom I talked that day on the way to the airport. It was obvious that she wanted with all her heart to forgive. She agonized over the effort. She wanted to forgive because it is a commandment and she wants to be an obedient child of her Heavenly Father. But she was challenged by the unfairness of it all. "Every day of our lives, we pay the price for his sin." Somewhere deep inside was an awareness that it did not serve justice for her to ignore her victims' rights in the matter—and that's what she believed she was being asked to do. She loved her Heavenly Father so much that she would not give up on the effort to obey in this ultimate way, but the wrestle persisted.

From the law of Moses and from knowing that it has been fulfilled, comes the deep down awareness that the need for justice is not unrighteous. On the contrary, the knowledge of the need for justice only makes us more grateful when we realize that we can receive justice. This good sister's error was her belief that the Plan of Happiness required of her to forfeit justice—to forfeit restitution. That is what was causing her pain. The great blessing of the law of Moses, perhaps the most important teaching of the "schoolmaster," is its teaching that restitution and restoration are among the great and precious promises of the Atonement.[4] We can trust our Heavenly Father and his son Jesus Christ to do whatever they have promised to do. They are gods of truth and cannot lie. The Savior has promised that not one jot or tittle of the law of Moses would pass away without his having fulfilled it. And the law of Moses includes justice; it includes full and infinite restitution.

It wasn't that this righteous struggling sister didn't love her

Father in Heaven enough to give him everything. She was serving him with all her heart. It wasn't that she was treasuring her victim's rights. It's just that she thought that she must pay the price forever and call it "no problem." She thought the requirement was to let mercy rob justice, and the spirit could not witness that justice is to be forfeited because it isn't. And so she struggled; not with rebellion, but with confusion. Confusion that can melt away with a careful scrutiny of the ancient God-given judgments. As Alma said so beautifully to his son Corianton:

"Now the work of justice could not be destroyed; if so, God would cease to be God. . . . God himself atoneth for the sins of the world, to bring about the plan of mercy, to appease the demands of justice, that God might be a perfect, just God, and a merciful God also" (Alma 42:13, 15).

Keep in mind that Corianton lived under the law of Moses. There can be no mistaking that he knew what justice meant. The law of Moses defines it. And the law of Moses was intended to teach us about both justice and mercy. It was intended to prepare us for the higher law.

And when we are prepared, we give our whole heart to our Father in Heaven because we love him and are grateful to him. We must humbly give our whole repentant soul—our broken heart and contrite spirit. That is the seeking of the restitution that is required of us—just as it was typified by the effort required of victims according to the law of Moses. At that point, through some ministering we can faithfully hope for, the result includes full and complete justice. Full and complete healing. We then are his, and he is our master forever. He has promised it, and it will be so; it was a part of the judgments. It is part of what we have to look forward to.

The law of Moses makes it clear that fear of paying the price forever need not be a barrier to forgiveness because we won't have to. It is true that in this world of trial and tribulation there will still be suffering and challenges connected to the sins of others as well as to our own sins; Satan is abroad in the land. But Christ has overcome the world, and has paid the infinite and necessary price to do so. When we express our great love for our Father in Heaven and accept the blessings of the Atonement we are recognizing that he will make us whole, that he will restore us, that he will make restitution on behalf of those who have sinned against us. Whatever that price is. And it seems reasonable to believe that the price may be different for you than for me—that it is personal and individual, that the sparrow does not fall without his notice. Exactly how that will occur is not ours to know. I know only that each of us who seeks wholeness will be made whole, and that which we have lost will be restored manyfold. Christ's atonement ransoms not only the sins we've committed but also the sins against us as well. It includes a complete satisfaction of our victims' rights.

Understanding this important fact of what the Atonement does can relieve us of the nagging struggle with fairness.

And the law of Moses makes it clear that there is no need to discount the pain of having been sinned against. Restitution is equivalent—at least. We don't have to follow society's lead to say "it is nothing." On the contrary, the greater we know our damage to be the more we value the Atonement. And the more we value the Atonement, the greater our love swells for that Savior who paid the price for full restitution, so that every jot and tittle of the law could be fulfilled.

I am reminded of the woman who had sinned and approached the Savior in the home of a Pharisee. She washed his feet with her tears. The Pharisee was offended that the Lord allowed it—she being a sinner well-known. The Lord answered with a parable:

"There was a certain creditor which had two debtors: the one owed five hundred pence, and the other fifty. And when they had nothing to pay, he frankly forgave them both. Tell me therefore, which of them will love him most? Simon answered and said, I suppose that he, to whom he forgave most. And he said unto him, Thou hast rightly judged" (Luke 7:41–43).

If Simon rightly judged regarding the debt we owe, is it not logical to believe the same truth about the debts that are owed to us? <u>The larger the debt he recompenses us for, the greater our love will be for him</u>. There is little benefit little benefit in claiming the wrong against us to be slight. Rather, when we give it full weight, we love the master all the more for healing us—for making us whole. *Yes!*

The act of discounting reaches its most devastating level in genuine denial. When denial becomes a coping mechanism for suffering, it will stand in the way of accepting the Atonement and receiving hope and therefore peace. Denial can be spiritually deadly. Who needs an atonement when one believes that he neither sins nor has been sinned against? And if one doesn't feel the need for the Atonement he will never feel that powerful love that led the woman to wash the Savior's feet with her tears. Denial is a prodigious obstacle to experiencing the love we need to reach toward the Savior. It's negative power notwithstanding, however, I mention denial only briefly here because one who copes in this way will probably not be the reader who has made it this far. Having been self-convinced that he has nothing to forgive, he will find this book at best uncomfortable.

These roadblocks—these barriers to forgiveness—can be insidious tools of the adversary. Satan delights to convince us that we will have to pay the price of our victimhood forever, and we'll have to claim that it is nothing. If he can make us *want* to think that it is nothing, he has won an even greater battle.

As long as such a mugging of justice is what we believe we

must face forgiveness will be difficult.

When, instead, we go back to the law of Moses to uncover the great gifts of restitution that the Atonement is ready to give us, we will have no more grudge to carry. We will know that in that great day of the Lord, our healing will be complete.

And if our healing will be complete, what of that third roadblock to forgiving? Not having been asked for forgiveness? Well, that difficulty vanishes. We, when we accept the Atonement, have sold our claim against our victimizer for enough to make us whole, or even more than whole. We no longer own the claim. Therefore, having received a check, we must write a paid in full receipt. The Lord, having paid us, is in possession of the cancelled check. The law of restitution is dead to us in terms of still anticipating payment or apology. It is, however, just as Paul said: established in that its requirements have been met.

"Do we then make void the law through faith? God forbid: yea, we establish the law" (Romans 3:31).

A dead issue to us, the apology is now due to our Savior who paid the debt to us. And isn't the justice beautifully infinite that the debt is now owed to the only being with the power to know the true heart of that debtor. He is the only being who can know whether that debtor's repentance is just words or if it is real and will bear the fruit meet for repentance (D&C 6:16).

The difficulties of forgiveness can melt away with the light that the law of Moses will shed on what the gift of the Atonement entails. Restoration, when sought, will happen. We will not have to pay the price for the sins of others. The price will be seen in its full magnitude and will not be discounted or denied. The begging for forgiveness will one day occur. It will be addressed, as it should be, to the great and glorious being who paid the price.

Notes

1. D&C 64:9.

2. C. S. Lewis, *The Weight of Glory,* ed. Walter Hooper (New York: Simon & Schuster, Touchstone Books, 1996), 133.

3. Spencer W. Kimball, *The Teachings of Spencer W. Kimball,* ed. Edward L. Kimball (Salt Lake City: Bookcraft, 1982), 204.

4. Alma 42 contains Alma's powerful response to Corianton, who struggled with a misunderstanding similar to that which I am describing here. Corianton, however, was persuaded by his misunderstanding to break the commandments, unlike the righteous sister whose story I am relating.

~ 5 ~

THE MASTER TEACHER

When examined with the light of the restored gospel, the law of Moses emerges as profound teaching—a truly amazing preparation for the Higher law. Its principles, internalized, are masterfully reassuring to those who have ears to hear and hearts to comprehend. It is an intensive drill that, properly and patiently worked, will give us a unique understanding of the Higher law.

When my husband was a resident physician in radiology, the chief of his department was an exceptionally caring man by the name of Dr. Earl R. Crowder. Mrs. Crowder too took an interest in Dr. Crowder's residents and often invited us to their home. Dr. Crowder had been a physics professor at Northwestern University before he came to LDS Hospital. Physics is a large part of radiology and, as we discussed one night around Mrs. Crowder's dinner table, mathematics is a large part of physics.

Most of the times in my life when I get into trouble, my mouth causes the trouble. That night at dinner was a perfect example.

"Oh, I hate math!" I said. "It's just too hard for me. I took beginning algebra when I was a senior in high school and the teacher was the freshman football coach. I was the only girl in the class and the rest of the class was the freshman football team. I don't know how I ended up in that class, but I never learned a thing. He explained everything in terms of split-T formations and other football plays. It was all one big tackle to me. I couldn't understand any part of it! That class was my only C in my school life (and even that was a gift.)"

If what I wanted was to be the center of attention, it was working. Dr. Crowder had a way of staring right through a person. There were several seconds of silence before he said, piercingly: "And you let it go at that?"

I laughed nervously. "Yes." Another few seconds of silence and it was I who felt compelled to break it: "Well, I have a mental block against math and I can get along without it. It's just too hard." Mrs. Crowder was smiling with knowledge of what was to come, and Dr. Crowder was staring at me with something obviously going on behind his eyes. Unknowingly I had just issued him a challenge he could not ignore.

"What do you do on Monday, Wednesday and Friday nights?"

"Well, I have nothing routine."

"Good. Now you do. From now on Monday, Wednesday, and Friday evenings will be spent in our basement and I will teach you mathematics. We will begin at six o'clock. Don't be late."

He changed the subject as if he had said nothing momentous and I was left wondering if he had said it at all. But the following Monday I showed up in Dr. Crowder's basement and began the most intensive—most careful step-by-step education that I have ever received. Dr. Crowder sat in a large chair (he was a big man) in front of a blackboard on the wall. It wasn't hard to figure out that I was not the first to stand at that board. I was given chalk and told to stand at the board and write as I was directed. He started by teaching me how to count. That sounds too fundamental, but as he drew my attention to the structure and reasons for numbering I immediately received insights on which I could build. For three hours each night, Dr. Crowder sat in that chair and I stood at the blackboard. As I progressed he gave me problems to solve and told me to show every step and to be careful about the placement and neatness of my work. He also told me to go as quickly as I could. As I worked—rushing along—he always noticed where I paused. And I was careful to pause as little as possible because that was a signal to him that it was a difficult concept and so wherever I paused, that concept would be what we would drill on for the next hour. I had his total attention. He never missed one of those pauses. As a result, my weaknesses became strengths. And that was true on both a specific and a general level. Mathematics never again intimidated me. In fact, I came to relish it as a way of thinking. I was still in college at the time, and for a while I even flirted with becoming a math major. I had been taught by a master teacher, drilled in my weaknesses, and I was thereby required to build upon my strengths.

I often think of my evenings with Dr. Crowder as I strive to live the gospel. I can't help but make the comparison because I feel certain the Lord is observing me as I pause. And, like the time at the blackboard, I feel a drill coming on.

The Lord has taught the same way throughout the ages. The ancient children of Israel on their way out of the slavery in Egypt were introduced to a potential for which they were not yet ready. They were given the invitation to go to the mountain—to go where God was (Exodus 19). They paused at the foot of mountain, unable to run to "the fountain of all righteousness" (1 Nephi 2:9). It was one of history's most prodigious pauses. For anyone as familiar as I am with pauses, it is not hard to feel the inevitability of the coming drill.

The Lord is the master teacher. He gives all of his children his full attention as we take the steps and show our work reaching toward the charity that is the higher law. He watches us. He sees us pause. He knows our difficulties and he drills us on the steps we must understand to solve the problems of progress.

The ancient children of Israel were the beneficiaries of attentive and painstaking teaching. The law of Moses was given to them because as they camped in the wilderness they paused at the opportunity they were given to become "a kingdom of priests, and an holy nation" (Exodus 19:6)—a state of being that had been enjoyed by their preslavery ancestors—a state of being that would result in peace and productivity for any generation of Israelites. And when they paused, God gave them—not a substitute—but a *preparatory* law. It was not a law designed to conform to their weaknesses, but designed to, over time, turn their weaknesses into strengths. It was appropriate that Paul called it a schoolmaster. It was a drill of the fundamentals. It was intended to bring them to acceptance of the Savior's atoning sacrifice.

As latter-day apostles of Jesus Christ have said so well: "The Lord . . . determined that he would give the tribes a preparatory course of lesser commandments upon which they could build an acceptance of the higher laws."[1]

"Thus it is crucial to understand that the law of Moses was . . . never intended to be something apart or separated from and certainly not something antagonistic to, the gospel of Jesus Christ. It was more elementary than the full gospel—thus its schoolmaster's role in bringing people to the gospel—but its purpose was never to have been different from the higher law. Both were to bring people to Christ."[2]

We who are members of the church are also the children of Israel (D&C 103:17), and if we find ourselves, as most of us do, hesitating when it comes to living fully the higher law—that is to say pausing when it comes to having a broken heart and contrite spirit, particularly when it comes to forgiving those who have trespassed against us, then we must surely benefit from studying the "preparatory course"—the drill given to our fathers.

With Robert J. Matthews, "I get nervous when I hear people criticize the law of Moses as though it were a bad law."[3] Mosiah made it clear that it is a "correct law" given by God. We call it a "lesser law" not because it is in any way flawed or loopholed, but because it contains lesser commandments and is administered by the lesser priesthood. As Brother Matthews points out: lesser does not mean that it is not a good priesthood. But it was a drill. It was intended to teach us fundamentals.

Because the Jews did not "remain at the blackboard" and do the drill as it was given, they didn't understand it, and so they had difficulty applying the fundamentals to the higher law when that law was given them. If they had lived the law the Lord's way, with the understanding that it should point them toward his fulfillment of it, they would have been ready when he came. But they had distorted and polluted the law. It was as if they hoped to become expert at solving a new problem by relentlessly practicing the wrong math facts.

The Lord had warned the Israelites of just such a danger. He talked symbolically of those who would try to improve on the simple judgments that the Lord had given them as a mode of worship.

"And if thou wilt make me an altar of stone, thou shalt not build it of hewn stone: for if thou lift up thy tool upon it, thou hast polluted it" (Exodus 20:25).

The Lord issued this warning just prior to giving them the drill that would prepare them to accept the atoning sacrifice of their Savior. He told them to leave the stone of their altar plain and unpolluted. It was a symbolic and prophetic caution not to make "improvements" on what the Lord requires of us. The warning went unheeded. The Israelites lifted their tool upon the law and polluted it.[4]

The end result in the ancient homeland of the Israelites was that the law was largely a failure. They didn't understand it and they were not brought to Christ. For them, the drill of the law had not been a success. It was a failure not of the drill, but of the students. When the Messiah came there was only a small fraction of the Jews who were prepared to value and worship him.

For the branch that went over the wall however (Genesis 49:22), the law was understood and not forgotten. It is to the people of the Book of Mormon we must look to see the success of the drill. Again, it is Abinadi, with his dying breath, who makes that success clear and expresses his profound understanding of the purpose of the law of Moses.

"Therefore there was a law given them, yea, a law of performances and of ordinances, a law which they were to observe strictly from day to day, to keep them in remembrance of God and their duty towards him. But behold, I say unto you, that all these things were types of things to come" (Mosiah 13:30–31).

In the Book of Mormon we have a record of people who, "stood at the blackboard" and relished their preparation for the higher law. In fact, their understanding led to such a faith in Christ that Nephi could already pronounce his people "alive in Christ," (2 Nephi 25:25) and Benjamin could declare the people in his congregation to be "born of him and . . . his sons and his daughters" (Mosiah 5:7).

It had to be an understanding of the higher law that would have made Nephi and his supporters "alive in Christ" and Benjamin and his hearers "born of Him." The higher law is the law of the broken heart and the contrite spirit. It is governed by the higher priesthood and it brings ultimate blessings. Just as some have called the law of Moses "the law of lesser commandments," we could call the higher law the law of greater commandments.

Nevertheless, it is important that we remember that as a drill, as a preparation, *the law of Moses is not flawed.* Granted, it is incomplete in terms of extending salvation, but it was always intended to be only the drill. It was never intended to be the fruition of the principles, but more like the exercise of an introduction to them.

It would, for another example, take long hours of exercise to make some of us ready to participate in an athletic event because our bodies are not fit to play. The exercise would not be the game itself, but would be an important preparation for our being able to play the game. Exercise may only be a preparatory law, but for most of us a significant one. It is crucial, however, that we do the exercises properly—neither taking shortcuts nor overdoing them—or fitness will not be achieved.

The law of Moses was meant to help us grasp and be converted to the fundamentals that will prepare us to have a broken heart and contrite spirit. For those that lived the law in an unadulterated fashion, it was the drill of those principles that are *foundation* for what we call "the higher law." As the psalmist said so beautifully, "The law of the Lord is perfect, converting the soul" (Psalm 19:7).

It is a testimony to the power of the exercise that King Mosiah bears when he says:

"The laws which have been given you by our fathers, . . . are correct, and . . . were given them by the hand of the Lord" (Mosiah 29:25).

That same respect and reverence for the law of Moses is essential if we have hope of learning from it. Still in our day, we can use the ancient schoolmaster to bring us to Christ.

Notes

1. Mark E. Petersen, *Moses, Man of Miracles* (Salt Lake City: Deseret Book 1978), 100.

2. Jeffrey R. Holland, *Christ and the New Covenant* (Salt Lake City: Deseret Book, 1997), 147.

3. Robert J. Matthews, *Selected Writings of Robert J. Matthews* (Salt Lake City: Deseret Book, 1999), 186.

4. Elder Jeffrey R. Holland describes the pollution this way: "We can be certain that Jesus was perfectly obedient to the spirit and the letter of the law of Moses. It was the law of the 'church' and the law of his people during his lifetime. It was spiritually based, it had fundamental elements of the gospel, and in its purity it was to lead to the holier law and higher priesthood. But he did not feel obliged to abide by the myriad additions, addendums, commentaries, and ultimately false insertions into the law that had been added in more than a thousand years of what was at best uninspired argument and at worst flagrant apostasy. The Torah, or five books of Moses, would have been perfectly known and accepted by Christ, at least in their pure and original form. What would give him grief would be the instructions and traditions added to the Torah" (*Christ and the New Covenant*, 147, 148).

~ 6 ~

FAITH AND PATIENCE

I stand all amazed at the Atonement. And I mourn at how long it took me to realize that the law of Moses could be my own schoolmaster—that I too am a child of Israel. But now that I understand the lesson (and surely many of you are way ahead of me on this next point) everything in the scriptures testifies to me of wholeness and healing—of restitution and restoration. Everything. Of course Christ said it should.[1] I look now, especially at the story of Job. His saga is all about the Atonement that was to come. Job was a victim, and in time was healed. Job received restitution. And Job is Everyman.

The book of Job begins with a scene in heaven where Satan is told that he will have power in the life of Job, but will not have the power to take Job's life. Neither Job's physical life nor his spiritual life is Satan's to command. Job's free agency is not dethroned by the marauding influence of the adversary.

Satan takes seriously this opportunity to destroy Job's well-being, and Job loses his fortune, his family, and his health. Job's friends gather to "comfort" him and blame him. If only he were doing everything right, his friends tell him, he would not be suffering so. But Job refuses to absorb the guilt and the hopelessness. He declares that he knows that he will be redeemed. And indeed, in the end, he is redeemed. Satan, who with malice victimized Job, is far from triumphant. Job received at least double restoration for all that he lost. In many matters, he received ten times or more than what he lost.

The reason that the story of Job is important is that Job really is Everyman. There really was a council in heaven (Abraham 3:23). The Lord did allow Satan to have a considerable amount of power to present opposition in this mortal sphere,[2] and Satan really does rob us—sometimes of loved ones, sometimes of prosperity, sometimes of health. And we really do—all of us—sometimes have friends like Job did, friends who will tell us that we must have deserved it, or we must have done something wrong, or if we would only this or only that—then we might extricate ourselves from the grip of misfortune.

But we must be wise as Job was, we must refuse to absorb the disparagement of others. Job rejected the self-focus his friends offered. Sad as his misfortunes made him and weak as he sometimes became, he maintained faith and hope and commitment. He refused to curse God and die spiritually. He understood (better than most of us do) what the blessings of the Atonement would be. And he trusted!

"I am as one mocked of his neighbor, who calleth upon God, and he answereth him . . . Though he slay me, yet will I trust in him" (Job 12:4; 13:15).

People talk about the patience of Job but his story is about more than just garden-variety patience. It is about faith and trust (or else what was he being patient for?). It is about earthly tribulation and the God that has overcome it (or else where is his faith and trust placed?). It is about restitution and healing. It is, like all of scripture, about the Atonement.

Indeed it was the first principle of the gospel that enabled Job's patience. Faith in the Lord Jesus Christ made patience possible for

Job. And make no mistake; it will make it possible for us as well. After all is said and done, there is a wait for the complete restitution and restoration, notwithstanding the love and peace we can feel right now if the faith is present. God's timetable is not our own and this sphere of trial and tribulation must be endured to the end. Patience comes from faith and trust in God's promises, faith that, as Paul reminded the Hebrews, "it was impossible for God to lie" (Hebrews 6:18). And the law is correct, and perfect. And Christ promised that he would fulfill every jot and tittle of the law of Moses. We must have faith in the Lord Jesus Christ, and he will restore to us all that we have lost! Paul reminds us that we must be "followers of them who through *faith and patience* inherit the promises" (Hebrews 6:12; emphasis added). Paul listed a great number of our scriptural heroes who had much to endure, but who, like Job, ultimately received the blessed fulfillment of the promises of the Lord (Hebrews 11). *My favorite chapter in the NT!*

Patience can be difficult. Patience is as challenging as it is necessary. As Elder Neal A. Maxwell said during the October 2002 general conference, "Regarding trials, including of our faith and patience, there are no exemptions—only variations."[3]

Only faith will bring patience, and only patience will bring peace.

There are those who believe that a call for patience is just another way of telling us to discount the wrong done to us, but patience is not the same as saying 'no problem.' Elder Maxwell pointed out in his beautiful address on patience, "Patience is not indifference. Actually, it means caring very much but being willing, nevertheless, to submit to the Lord and to what the scriptures call 'the process of time.'"[4]

Paul and Moroni both referred to *hope* as being the anchor of the soul (Hebrews 6:19; Ether 12:4). During our period of faith and patience we do indeed need an anchor. That anchor must be hope. The period can be long and hard and we are in danger of drifting from our endurance. We must not weary in well-doing. Hope must anchor us, must feed us spiritually as we carry on with life's ordeal. It was hope that anchored and fed Job.

We must remember, as Job did, that the Lord did not leave us without warning. Our creator told us over and over that there would be pain. He warned and still warns us that Satan would be and is abroad in the land. But he gave us the hope of his great and precious promises and he said:

"In your patience possess ye your souls" (Luke 21:19).

What if we *do* weary in well-doing? What if we *don't* develop faith and patience enough to feel the hope that can anchor our souls?

Well, we don't have to *accept* the Lord's payment as satisfaction of our victims' rights. We have our agency to choose despair over hope. The Lord died to guarantee that right. But if we don't accept the sacrifice of our Savior, we have reason to despair indeed. We will have to pay to the uttermost farthing for our own sins—our own victimization of others (D&C 19:16–19). Perhaps the only way we will even begin to be able to meet the requirements of the law (if we reject the payment Christ has made) will be for us to be sold to Satan to pay our debt. As Alma said to Corianton:

"O my son, whosoever will come may come and partake of the waters of life freely; and whosoever will not come the same is not compelled to come; but in the last day it shall be restored unto *him* according to *his* deeds.

"Do not suppose, because it has been spoken concerning restoration, that ye shall be restored from sin to happiness. . . .

"Therefore, my son, see that you are merciful unto your brethren; deal justly, judge righteously, and do good continually; and if ye do all these things then shall ye receive your reward; yea, ye shall have mercy restored unto you again; ye shall have justice restored unto you again" (Alma 42:27; 41:10, 14; emphasis added).

Christ did not come to destroy the law but to fulfill it. He gave the eye for the eye, and the tooth for the tooth, the wound for the wounding. No matter how large our damages, they are paid when we accept the Atonement in both word and deed, with a broken heart and contrite spirit. He sees for us when our eyes have been taken. He gives us power when our power has been thwarted. He makes a path for us when our path has been blocked. He satisfies the requirements of the law not only by giving us his gift of healing and restitution but also by taking the punishment attached to every law by giving his sinless self to suffer and to die. So he paid doubly—even infinitely—both by damages and by punishment. In Gethsemane and on Calvary he both gave restitution and suffered the mischief consequence as well. Not one of our debts was disregarded. And all of us have been, and will be repaid much more than ever we could be owed by others. Our salvation is thoroughly dependent upon our accepting that. Or, in other words, of us it is required that we forgive all men.

To accept Christ is to accept his fulfillment of the law—or in other words, to accept his payment for sins—both ours against others and others' against us. His mercy for *our* misdeeds is given *because* of that dual acceptance. His recognition of our repentance comes only when our love is profound, our hearts are broken, our spirits are contrite, and the restitution that others owe us is marked paid-in-full as far as we're concerned because we have accepted the payment of Christ's atonement for those debts. It is a payment that he has promised will "cause [us] to be thoroughly healed" (Exodus 21:19). We have no more claim against those who owe us restitution because the claim either has been or will be satisfied by the Savior. We call it forgiving others when we acknowledge that the debt has been paid. If we haven't done that we have not really accepted Christ because we haven't accepted his payment. Therefore, forgiveness of others is not just a *condition* of our receiving what Paul called the adoption by Jesus Christ to himself, forgiveness *is* our receipt of that adoption. We beg forgiveness of our sins by pleading for him to pay our debts payable, and by calling our debts receivable paid in full. That is, by definition, our acceptance of the sacrifice of the Son of God. And if that acceptance is timely and heartfelt, accompanied by honored covenants, we become his sons and his daughters (Mosiah 5:7).

Sometimes we like to think of our obedience and good works as being the way that we accept the sacrifice of our Savior, and certainly our good works are *evidence* of that acceptance because our love and gratitude will lead to keeping his commandments.

"I will show thee my faith by my works" (James 2:18).

The actual acceptance, however, is not our behavior weighed on a scale. It is a broken heart and contrite spirit that lead us to humble, grateful works. Acceptance of Christ is to no longer press for debts owed us, and to no longer carry the guilt of debts we owe. This miraculous acceptance leaves us overwhelmed with obedient love. But, as Paul reminded us: "by the deeds of the law there shall no flesh be justified" (Romans 3:20).

We go to him because we no longer value our own will above our servant relationship to him, and he makes us instead his very sons and daughters. It is not just restoration. It is not just double or treble or even ten times damages. It is infinite restitution.

The law of Moses tells us what the Atonement does and will do. We still don't know *how* it is done. But trust and patience makes that knowledge not important. The magnitude of the *what* overwhelms us with hope.

Far from the law of Moses being the antithesis of the love of Christ, it makes that love so much more real and therefore, so much more comforting. It makes it possible to have the patience with which to possess our souls. It gives us hope—the hope that anchors our souls.

"But if we hope for that we see not, then do we with patience wait for it" (Romans 8:25).

Notes

1. John 5:39; Moses 6:62–63.

2. Moses 4:21: "And thou shalt bruise his heel."

3. Neal A. Maxwell, "Encircled in the Arms of His Love," *Ensign,* November 2002, 17.

4. ———, "Patience," in *1979 Devotional Speeches of the Year* (Provo, Utah: Brigham Young University Press, 1980), 215.

~ 7 ~

WHAT A GIFT!
RECEIVING IT IS
ALL ABOUT LOVE

If you were to ask most folks what the Atonement means to them, you would get an answer like this:

"It means that Christ died to atone for my sins. It means he is my personal savior."

It might be different in language, but it would be similar in content. And as important as that is to know, it is incomplete. We need to understand what the law of Moses teaches: Christ is the Savior of those who have sinned against us because he will restore us and make us whole as would be our right under the law. He leaves no price unpaid. He rescues *us* from our debts to those who have suffered for our behavior because he will heal those whom we have wronged—knowingly or unknowingly. He restores us by healing us from the damages *we* have received at the hands of *others*. He ransoms us from being sold to be a servant of Satan because he makes the payment of debts for which we are unable to make restitution. He fulfills the law of justice by making us fully whole from the damages *we* have sustained—knowingly or unknowingly—at the hands of those who have in any way abused us. I have sold my victimizer to him in order to receive the payment that will "cause [us] to be thoroughly healed" (Exodus 21:19).

That additional answer taught us by the law of Moses is

cause for hope indeed!

51

surely not even complete at that. We can't know, of course, every beautiful thing the Lord has in store for us. But what we can know brings us immeasurable comfort.

The Atonement thoroughly heals! It gives the restitution that the law requires. It restores us. It fulfills the justice requirements of the law. Many of us have been walking around believing that we will be required to give mercy without receiving justice. But as Alma said so pleadingly to his son: "the work of justice could not be destroyed" (Alma 42:13), and as James Talmage said so eloquently in our dispensation: "Justice is not to be dethroned by mercy."[1]

Of course, it seems less difficult to understand the kind of mercy that we ourselves want to receive: the mercy that means on condition of repentance we won't reap the justice that would be enforceable *against* us. That's the kind of mercy that is more commonly stressed, so we tend to be grateful for that. We are "amazed" that Christ suffered to pay *our* debts, even though we don't focus on what those debts are. We ignore (or maybe never realized) that the price he paid included restitution to those we have hurt and to whom we are thereby indebted. He paid the debt to the law—the debt that *we* owe. We just don't focus on our victims enough to realize what that means. We forget that we have a debt of restitution to pay to those whom we have hurt and that he has paid that debt for us. To remember it would be to be overwhelmed. But that is the truth of it. What a relief of our guilt! Those we have hurt can receive restitution beyond which we could ever give them. This very mission was the one Christ cited when he announced his Messiahship in the synagogue in Nazareth:

"He hath sent me to heal the brokenhearted, to preach deliverance to the captives, and recovering of sight to the blind, to set at liberty them that are bruised" (Luke 4:18).

The actual language: "recovering of sight to the blind" seems to be a direct reference to the judgments. Christ will give the eye for the eye in the precise intent of the law: He will restore sight.

When we learn to love others we desperately want that restoration for them. We are overcome with guilt and sadness at having hurt them. It is all about love. In fact, it is *only* when we feel that love that we understand that particular pain. When we do feel it, the knowledge that Christ can heal those whom we have hurt is absolutely and resplendently comforting. The people we *Yes!* love won't have to suffer because of *our* sins anymore.

The comfort that we receive comes from believing in the promise of Christ himself. It is part of understanding what he meant when he gave his own statement of his mission.

"He healeth the broken in heart, and bindeth up their wounds" (Psalm 147:3).

Christ pays the price both for us and to us. We need love to show gratitude for both of those payments. Love is fundamental to accepting the healing of our own wounds received at the hand of others.

Although our Savior stands ready to give us restitution as well as restitution to those whom we have hurt, we will not be coerced into accepting it (Alma 42:27). And it is, of course, entirely possible to know that restitution is available, and still reject the payment. It's all about love. Or the lack of it.

Christ, out of his great love, is willing to give us restitution for every way in which we have been damaged. He stands ready to satisfy our every claim in our role as a victim, every debt we are owed. It seems, then, that any reason we might have for turning away from accepting that loving payment is rooted in our unwillingness to return the love. Accepting the Atonement is all about love. Obeying the commandment to love is the whole key to that acceptance. Love of God or love of our neighbor would stand to cancel out any reason we might have for turning away from full acceptance of the atonement of Christ—which explains, of course, why it is on these two laws that all of the law and prophets rest.

Still we tend to back away from the commandment to love. Some, for instance, might not want to accept the Savior's restitution because they feel that they know best how their victimizer should be held responsible and they, therefore, don't want to give up their perceived role in enforcing punishment. To these folks, it's worth not having their damages paid just so they feel they have a controlling role, illusory as that feeling is.

"I know him better than anyone else and my forgiveness is not what he needs. He needs to pay for this. He needs to be taught a lesson. It isn't about healing *me*. It's about paying for what he did. It won't do him any good to think he hoodwinked me. He needs to suffer for a good long while. Believe me I know what I'm talking about."

This sort of desire to 'play God' is blasphemy on the face of it—making it a grievous sin—showing a complete lack of trust in the Savior's wisdom. The sin, however, would be completely prevented by loving God with all your heart, might, mind and strength. Because that kind of love brings trust with it—trust in both judgment and payment. Because, as Solomon understood so well, "There is a way that seemeth right unto a man, but the end thereof are the ways of death" (Proverbs 16:25). Or in other words, we must trust in the Lord because we know and understand so little that we are apt to make choices that would separate us from the perfect love that God desires to give us. Paul said it differently: "We see through a glass, darkly" (1 Corinthians 13:12).

Perhaps the most frequent reason for turning away from the Savior's offer of restoration (when we know it is available) is ingratitude. Not being grateful enough to value that payment can be the root problem. Because this state of affairs is so all-pervasive, it will be dealt with extensively in a chapter of its own. For the present, however, we need only realize that ingratitude—in its many permutations—is also an indication of a lack of love.

Perhaps the most virulent reason that some do not wish to accept the Savior's payment of their victim's rights is that they are consumed with hate. Hate is more than just the absence of love; it is an active rejection of love.

And the simple *absence* of love is rarely the problem in a victims' rights situation. The difficulty is much more apt to be an active *rejection* of it. Turning away from the Lord's payment of the debts owed to us is time and again a symptom of outright hatred. We hatefully want our "pound of flesh" from our victimizer. We turn away from restitution because we want not just payment, not even just punishment, but revenge. Our hate for our enemy can be greater than our desire to simply be free of the pain that our enemy has inflicted upon us. This happens when our anger has consumed and reduced to ashes our sense of equivalence in damages. It is a return to a kind of barbarism. It is valuing settling of the score above settling of the damages.

"I'm not going to let him get off that easily! I don't care if he is sorry! He should be sorry. I don't care if I ever get a nickel back of what he cheated me out of. I want him to pay! I want him hurt! I want to watch him suffer for what he put me through. I want to be the one who pulls the switch. I don't want him repenting and getting off scot-free."

Rarely, though, are we so open as to admit to such vengeful hatred. We often continue to claim that it is simply restitution we want. When we know that we can receive restitution from the Lord, however, simple payment is not really what our anger is about; it is about hate. And interestingly, the Lord's promises make our anger for and hatred of our victimizer groundless because full payment is available. And if there are no grounds for our anger and hatred, it is plainly a product of our own malevolence.

I believe that it is this hatred—this groundless anger—that the Lord is addressing when he says in the Sermon on the Mount: "Whosoever is angry with his brother without a cause shall be in danger of the judgment" (Matthew 5:22). For us, anger is "without a cause" because Christ himself will make the requisite restitution. Far from a justification of some kinds of anger, I see this verse now as reminding us that we will not be ultimately damaged by the behavior of others, therefore, our anger is always "without a cause." In the Joseph Smith Translation, the words "without a cause" do not appear, which makes the language clearer for those who do not understand the law.

Because all anger is without a cause, the Lord stressed that hatred must be done away: "Ye have heard that it hath been said, Thou shalt love thy neighbor, and hate thine enemy. But I say unto you, Love your enemies" (Matthew 5:43, 44).

If we, with real intent, accept the atonement of Christ, we will necessarily give up hatred.

Arrogance and ingratitude and, worst of all hate, must be chipped away with an effort to love our enemies because "he that forgiveth not his brother his trespasses standeth condemned before the Lord; for there remaineth in him the greater sin" (D&C 64:9).

That greater sin is rejection of the Atonement as payment.

Although all of us struggle with obstacles before accepting the Atonement, it is absolutely necessary to give every effort to eradicating those barriers in our hearts if we are to receive the great blessing of "peace in this world, and eternal life in the world to come" (D&C 59:23). Those barriers can only be torn down with love. Until we at least *begin* to tear them down, the barriers can be absolute. Accordingly, for those of us who understand the great barriers, it is not surprising to hear the Lord say that the two great commandments in the law are to love God and love one another. It is not for the pleasure of God or for our neighbor that we must love them. It is for our own good.

Without love we are walled up from accepting any part of the Atonement. Without love, we must essentially be sold to Satan to pay our own debts.

In the awareness of this principle we can see how utterly destructive it was when the Jews "lifted their tool" upon the law and inserted attitudes and standards of behavior that encouraged hatred of their victimizers and a belief more in self than in a Savior.[2] The plan was that restitution was to be received with love, not with anger. Mercy was always an important principle. The law of Moses was eye for eye, wound for wound, all right, but it was never originally intended to be hate for hate. And that distortion stopped the drill from preparing the Jews for the higher law.

Not that the Jews are alone in this distortion. Each of us finds ways to avoid loving every day. But Christ told those Pharisees, who thought their knowledge to be all-important, that they should search the scriptures; that the ancient scriptures themselves were "they which testify of me" (John 5:39). That is still true today. The law of Moses is still available to "search." It can lead us toward love and motivate us to eliminate arrogance, ingratitude, and hate from our dispositions.

With or without that search, it is a yielding of arrogance, ingratitude, and hate, and substituting an overriding reach toward love that will open up the gates of heaven and give us peace.

Notes

1. James E. Talmage, *Jesus the Christ* (Salt Lake City: The Church of Jesus Christ of Latter-day Saints, 1981), 392.

2. We share this danger with our ancestors. Belief in self instead of in the Savior is encouraged in our society and must be resisted.

~ 8 ~

A ROLE TO PLAY

A dear friend, whose thought process I respect, was sharing my delight in the law of Moses and the way it teaches the reassuring doctrine of restitution.

"But how can we be so certain that the restitution will come as part of the acceptance of Christ—part of the repentance process, part of the broken heart and the contrite spirit? Why is it not just as possible that restitution could come as part of the resurrection process: given to all mortal beings certainly and unconditionally?"

The question is a valid one. It is worth examining the reasons for asserting that restitution comes with the broken heart and the contrite spirit.

We are required, as part of our accountability as victimizers, to make restitution to the best of our ability right here in the mortal sphere—right now in terms of priority. That effort is *prima facie* evidence that our repentance is real. And yet, important as that effort is, our outcome is feeble. We cannot thoroughly make up for pain and suffering. We are inadequate to thoroughly heal. Perhaps the necessity of our attempt to restore wholeness to someone is a symbol of our acknowledgement that the restitution has been and will be made by Christ, the only being with knowledge enough, power enough, and love enough, to make restitution truly complete. Our effort does create a beautiful and reassuring symbol—an educating exercise that can lead us to an appreciation of the awesomeness of what the Lord can and will do, but in terms of absolute effectiveness, a symbol is probably all it is.

What the law calls *thorough* healing cannot be a condition of our paltry efforts to accomplish it. It is infinitely comforting, then, to know that it is the Atonement that fulfills the law of restitution, leaving me with this powerful piece of information: when we have sinned against another, our victim's healing does not depend upon *our* repentance—our need to make the effort notwithstanding.

The answer as to whether or not the healing is dependent on our victims' *own* repentance became, for a time after the conversation with my friend, less certain. That which had seemed obvious to me became something for which I needed evidence. Does the blessing of restoration from all hurts come like the resurrection, or maybe even as part of the resurrection? Do victims' rights in general fall into that category? Has restitution the same inevitability as the resurrection or is it more a matter of availability?

The purpose of this earthly trial ("and we will prove them herewith"[1]) is to see if we will keep the commandments of God in this our second estate—an estate where victimization is abroad in the land. In other words, being a victim is part of the human condition—part of the environment to which we were sent. Just as we talked about in chapter one, agency came with the inevitability that mortals would wound one another. The oppositional environment (which Lehi says is so essential to making the choices we are sent here to make) is evidenced and perpetuated by our victimizing one another. Some oppositional alternatives may be created by the ripple effects of violations of the will of God that happened generations before our time. We are all victims of far more than we know. But Lehi said that the Atonement makes us "free forever . . . to act for [our]selves and not to be acted upon" (2 Nephi 2:26).

This statement is an echo of the psalmist: "Great peace have they which love thy law: and nothing shall offend them" (Psalm 119:165). We will not feel acted upon if we love the law because we can be free from worry about lasting effects of offenses against us. To continue with Lehi:

"And they are free to choose liberty and eternal life, through the great Mediator of all men, or to choose captivity and death, according to the captivity and power of the devil" (2 Nephi 2:27).

We are captives of our victimizers and the power of the devil as long as we are being acted upon—as long as we are taking offense and feeling the lack of justice.

"And now, my sons, I would that ye should look to the great Mediator, and hearken unto his great commandments; and be faithful unto his words, *and choose eternal life . . . And not choose eternal death . . . which giveth the spirit of the devil power to captivate, to bring you down to hell*" (2 Nephi 2:28, 29; emphasis added).

The "spirit of the devil" causes us to victimize one another. It fashions residuals for centuries and millennia. I believe that Lehi's words teach us that we can *choose* whether to accept the payment of the great Mediator or let the "spirit of the devil" (the actions of those who have victimized us) bring us down to hell. That is the choice. Will we wallow in the hell our victimizers have inflicted upon us, or will we choose liberty and eternal life by accepting the thorough healing of the atonement of Christ? Our victimizers are not given the right to make that choice for us. They can inflict pain and suffering, but as Job understood, they cannot choose to take our spiritual life—only we can do that. The exciting comfort of what we learn from the law of Moses is that choosing the great Mediator—far from being a choice to *sacrifice* our victims' rights—is also a choice to *receive* victims' rights: full and complete restitution, restoration and healing. By choosing Christ we "lay hold upon *every* good thing" (Moroni 7:19; emphasis added). I am not suggesting that it would not be worth it if we had to give up justice to accept Christ, I am offering the magnificent information that we will receive even justice when we accept Christ.

Receiving that justice takes place when Christ sees our love as sincere, and pronounces the fullness of the Atonement on our efforts.

When the great Jehovah gave the law of Moses, he promised that if we would love him and love our families enough to want to serve him as our master forever, that he would "bring [us] unto the judges" (Exodus 21:6). There is so much portent in that promise. Why do we have to go the judges, and why would we need our master to be by our side there? The message of the law of Moses is that we both owe debts and are owed them. The judges will establish both kinds of debt, just as was required in ancient Israel. Judgments will have to be ruled upon and handed down. Witnesses are needed. A determination of what restitution will cause us to be thoroughly healed (in the language of the law) will have to be made.

But Christ will, when we have shown our desire to serve him, go with us to the judges. Lehi calls Christ the great Mediator. He has also been called our advocate. Interestingly, we ourselves, when we want to make a statement that is utterly trusted, have been heard to say: "As God is my witness."

When Christ the Mediator, the Advocate, the Witness, goes with us to the judges, it means, for one thing, that we will receive righteous judgment; for another thing—it means that he, himself, will pay for the settlement of that righteous verdict. That is the message of the Sermon on the Mount, of Amulek's beautiful sermon, of Alma's and Paul's profound promises: justice will be done. The law of Moses describes the order of it.

Jehovah began the section on justice as: "These are the judgments." With Christ by our side, when those judgments are witnessed to and handed down, *then* the victims' rights are both created and satisfied. As David said to Saul, "The Lord judge between me and thee, and the Lord avenge me of thee" (1 Samuel 24:12).

After we have become his forever because of our love for him and because of our broken heart and contrite spirit—then the victims' rights—every jot and tittle of them will be fulfilled. Whether it be in this life or in the life to come, whether it be a timely repentance for eternal life, or whether it be the clear choice between light and darkness that will have to be made at the end of the Millennium, we cannot go to the judges without an advocate, without a witness, without a mediator. And we cannot claim the right of a judgment that has not been awarded in our favor.

Restitution, therefore, must be a part of the judgment and not a part of the physical resurrection. As the Doctrine and Covenants teaches us, ultimately every knee will bow and every tongue confess that Jesus is the Christ, or there will be no power to receive even the telestial glory (D&C 76:109, 110). I believe that it is with that confession of his Messiahship that victims' rights will be satisfied—that is when he will go with us to the judges. What really is it that proves us if the righting of all wrongs is ours without a judgment? The law of Moses makes the judgment process clear—right down to the witnesses required.

If receiving victims' rights, that is to say the righting of all wrongs—every ripple of victimization that exists in our lives— were automatic at the bestowing of immortality, it would become something we could consider an "entitlement." Surely it is too tender a consolation for that to be the case. It is of course no more majestic than the resurrection itself, and yet it seems so individual, so personal, so enfolding, that coming as part of the judgment instead makes it sweeter. Restitution is somehow more joyful as a right that we are *given* by the witness of our master when he goes with us to the judges, instead of a right that we have de facto.

That restitution that we ourselves can neither give nor get settles on us (in one way or another) through the miracle of the Atonement. The vision both excites and eases us. We celebrate the Son. We awaken those who have been in darkness.

It is not a sense of entitlement that can bring us peace and joy, but a sense of trust. Knowing, as we do, that he has promised, as our master, that he will overcome the world—the fulfillment of our victims' rights—we can therefore rely upon it, just as David did with Saul.

Continuously the scriptures goad us to *trust*. One of my favorite passages in this regard is the closing of the book of Habakkuk—a prophet whom I would have loved to know and at whose feet I sit even now. Habakkuk was a contemporary of Lehi's. He was not honored with the assignment to leave for a promised land and he knew that the destruction of Jerusalem was coming. He struggled with patience. Nevertheless, trust was his message:

"Although the fig tree shall not blossom, neither shall fruit be in the vines; the labor of the olive shall fail, and the fields shall yield no meat . . . Yet I will rejoice in the Lord, I will joy in the God of my salvation. The Lord God is my strength, and he will make my feet like hinds' feet, and he will make me to walk upon mine high places" (Habakkuk 3:17–19).

I think of the trust Alma the Elder taught at the waters of Mormon (Mosiah 18). If we are willing to bear one another's burdens (make the symbolic effort to restore) then what have we against accepting the sacrifice of Christ who can do what we can-not—who can heal thoroughly and make the complete restitution that the law requires? Without that acceptance, we must pay to the uttermost farthing ourselves—even if it means being sold to Satan for our debt.

We go to the Lord in celebration of the dawn, and only in acknowledging the dawn do we fully awake. That is the message of the scriptures as Christ links forgiveness to being forgiven, over and over again.

Receiving thorough healing is part of the gladness of accepting Christ. Being a victim is a part of the human condition—part of the vicissitudes of mortality. Having this mortal life and its vicissitudes leave no damage and no debt owed or owing—and in fact having the experience accelerate our progress—I believe *that* requires the "choosing" of the charity. The acceptance of the sacrifice as payment; the acknowledgment of the Son rising, the celebration of the Son.

Note

1. Abraham 3:25.

～ 9 ～

GRATITUDE IS FUNDAMENTAL—
AGAIN

It is, as we have already pointed out, entirely possible to have studied the drill, to know what Christ's sacrifice can do for us—even to be willing to personally repent of our sins—and in spite of everything undervalue the love of the Lord Jesus Christ that has been manifest in all his great gifts to us. If we undervalue that love and those gifts, we will not be grateful for them. If we are not grateful for them—and I mean grateful for all of his gifts to us—we will develop neither the faith nor the patience to fully accept the form of payment that the Lord is prepared to make— for our own sins *or* for our victims' rights. The broken heart and the contrite spirit can only come about in the presence of absolute and unqualified thankfulness. Our gratitude is not an arbitrary requirement to serve God's personal needs. It serves *our* needs. Without it we cannot become exalted. Still we struggle with it.

Perhaps our lack of gratitude is, as suggested in an earlier chapter, a matter of impatience. It can be, like Steven Robinson suggests, a matter of disbelief.

"They may believe that the Church is true, that Jesus is the Christ, and that Joseph Smith was a prophet of God, while at the same time refusing to accept the possibility of their own complete forgiveness."[1]

Perhaps it is charity itself that presents a problem for some. And, sadly, for many of us at some times it can be a simple prefer- ence for self-pity—a treasuring up of our victim status—a deviant desire to feel unblessed.

Whatever the barriers that stand in the way of our being grate- ful for the Lord's love and sacrifice, the barriers that protect our pride and prevent our meek and reverent valuing of Jesus Christ, our fundamental priority must be to dismantle those barriers.

⌒

A wonderfully faithful young adult friend of mine came to me once with a question. She had been sitting in a circle of friends having a late night talk and the subject had got around to trusting their Father in Heaven. Each member of the group felt that they trusted him to give them the blessings that they desired, but they were all beginning to be impatient for some of them. My young friend knew that trust was what fostered patience and knowing the relationship of trust to patience led her to want to be sure of her trust. "What can we count on him to give us, Sister Rasband?"

The answer could be quickly given: "Whatever he's promised you."

I suppose it was given too quickly because it startled her with its simplicity. "But am I not promised all my righteous desires? Which of my desires are unrighteous?"

I wished that I could give her an unqualified *yes* to the first part of her question because I felt the question was rightly in first place. She was surely right regarding the ultimate truth, but I sensed that the question was not really about *ultimate* blessings.

"All your righteous desires? Well, yes," I said slowly and cau- tiously, "but not by a week from Tuesday." My eyebrows went up and I tilted my head a bit; she knew I was telling her not to be impatient. I went on. "As far as which desires are righteous—well, isn't that by definition desires that are in accordance with the will of the Lord and for which you are willing to do whatever is required?"

"But that's just it! How can I *know* the will of the Lord about my desires?" My head tilted again and we both smiled. It seems always to come down to that question. We are given the assignment to live in an uncertain mortal state. We can keep the commandments and have *some* certainty—at least about pitfalls the commandments would help us avoid. And we can receive the promptings of the Spirit and have direction in a given moment as to what we should do. But as to bonus blessings—our hearts' yearnings in addition to the information in the commandments and the direction of the spirit—we must trust in the ultimate. That which we would design for ourselves here on earth may or may not be included. We can be sure of the climax, but the denouement is not ours to know. It is somewhat like a good novel. If we know the author and see the strengths and weaknesses of the well-drawn characters in the plot, it may be clear to us how the book will end, but the twists and turns of how it gets there—that is still totally unpredictable, and well worth the read. Life is like that. If we are wise, we will find our testimony of the outcome comfort enough and not bemoan the unknowns as we go along.

One of my favorite hymns has come to be "Lead, Kindly Light" (*Hymns,* no. 97). John Henry Newman, who struggled with religious understanding his whole life, composed the lyrics. In this hymn, penned near the end of that life, he writes:

"Keep thou my feet; I do not ask to see the distant scene—one step enough for me. . . . I loved to choose and see my path; but now, lead thou me on!"

If we are of a mind to see the mortal, distant scene before we can accept the peace of the restoring gift of Christ's atonement, we will not know the glorious rest that our redemption (paid debts—receivable and payable) actually offers now. Information about the specifics of what is in store for us is not part of the peace. It might even stand in the way of it. We know only that he is a God of truth and cannot lie, and that therefore he will keep his promises. And it is hope for those "great and precious promises"[2] that anchors our souls. Without that hope, our souls will stay adrift in our uncertainty—an anxiety-producing state if ever there was one.

Our impatience makes us want to know and see our blessings now. Even though we know what happened to the prodigal son when he wanted his inheritance prematurely,[3] we too would often leave our father's protection to get immediate gratification. I think of Shakespeare's line about prayer: "My words go up, [but] my thoughts remain below."[4] When we are impatient, sometimes not even our words go up.

The same sort of surrender to appetite that cost Esau his birthright and the prodigal son his happy home may be what is interfering with our acceptance of and gratitude for the Atonement. We want to focus on *this* life (our desires remain below) and so, as Shakespeare said, we become like the person who "sells eternity to get a toy."[5]

Paul said it the most clearly of all: "If in this life only we have hope in Christ, we are of all men most miserable" (1 Corinthians 15:19). Our hope must focus on eternal life—not on the temporary trial we know here.

For some of us it is not so much a matter of impatience as it is disbelief. We can't be thankful for what we don't accept, and because the Atonement is a process beyond our understanding, we automatically reject it. We require intellectual understanding, and we mistrust the things of the Spirit. It is no matter that our understanding is primitive and inadequate; we limit our beliefs to whatever conforms to it. Foolish us.

It is not that God intends to keep us in the dark. He has promised that he will unfold the mysteries of the kingdom to us. It's just that the unfolding must happen line upon line and in accordance with our readiness and trust. The scriptures have several examples of this process and what is required to enter into it. Perhaps my favorite of these is the story of the brother of Jared. His faith has already enabled him to see the finger of the Lord—a blessing that he is thrilled to receive, but not one he has demanded. The blessing was a reward for faith in the *power* of the Lord's finger not faith that he could satisfy any curiosity (Ether 3:4). Had he been searching for a sign, the story of the Jaredites might have been quite different indeed. But the brother of Jared's great faith in the Lord's power secured for him not only the *power* of the finger but also a glimpse of it as well. The Lord then asks "Sawest thou more than this?" (Ether 3:9).

In the scriptures the word *see* is much more often associated with understanding than it is with physical sight. The Lord is asking the brother of Jared here if he understood what being able to see the Lord's body meant. And the brother of Jared innocently responds, "Nay; Lord show thyself unto me" (Ether 3:10). The Lord brings him back to the subject of comprehension: "Believest thou the words that I shall speak?" (Ether 3:11). And the brother of Jared makes the all-important statement of trust: "Yea, Lord, I know that thou speakest the truth, for thou art a God of truth, and canst not lie" (Ether 3:12). It is the same statement of faith that Enos made regarding the washing away of his guilt (Enos 1:6). It is the same statement of faith that Paul quoted Abraham as knowing (Hebrews 11:17). He is a God of truth and "canst not lie."

The Lord answered the brother of Jared that because he knew

these things he could not be kept outside of the veil. And the Lord proceeded to unfold the mysteries of the kingdom to the brother of Jared—some things so precious they could not be written.

If we want to receive the blessings of redemption and experience the gratitude that makes that possible, we must conquer our disbelief. We must get to the point where we know that God is a god of truth and cannot lie. We have evidence of it in our lives just as surely as our ancestors did in their being brought out of Egypt. We must focus on being grateful for our blessings and let that focus lead us to perfect trust. He, in essence, asks every one of us "Believest thou the words that I will say?" And every one of us must learn to answer, "Yea, Lord, I know that thou speakest the truth, for thou . . . art a God of truth, and canst not lie" (Ether 3:12). Knowing *those* things will give us the patience to possess our souls. And the mysteries of the joy of the Atonement will open up to us. We should all cry out in our prayers: "Lord I believe, help thou my unbelief."[6]

⌒

The Lord said that there are really only two things with which he takes offense: the second thing is disobedience, but the number one offense comes when we "confess not his hand in all things" (D&C 59:21). The number one offense is not acknowledging his charity. Isn't that interesting?

We like to believe that we are responsible for our own blessings. We often don't want to acknowledge his hand at all, let alone in "all things." Pride is what we strive to preserve for ourselves and for others. Pride is a denial of charity; a denial, as Moroni so often warned against, of the gift and power of God. Rejection of charity is the grossest form of ingratitude for it, and will be a prodigious barrier to our receiving the peace of knowing that restitution is available. Restitution is, after all, to be received by all of us as charity from the Savior. Perhaps an allegory will underscore the essential nature of charity and our acceptance of it:

Let's say we want to move into an exclusive residential community, a neighborhood of "many mansions." The only problem is that we don't have the money for the purchase of the mansion or for the homeowner's dues, which must also be paid up front.

We do, however, have a dear friend who lives in the community and who wants us for a neighbor, so much so, that he is willing to pay for our mansion and also for our homeowner's dues. He does say, however, that he will only do so if we will give him whatever we do have. And that has to be *everything* we do have, including our accounts receivable.

The problem is that we are uncomfortable with the arrangement our loving friend proposes. We don't want to move into that grand community feeling abjectly poor. And we don't want to be a charity case. We want to go in there holding our head up high and feeling like we earned it ourselves. Our friend tells us that charity is the only way we will ever make it because we will never have enough to make it on our own.

"But," we argue with him, "if we got into that community having given up all we have, without any of our own riches, what do we really have when we get there? A big empty house." Our friend assures us that we will have beautiful furnishings and that he will see to it that we will have wealth and status beyond our wildest imaginings.

"I don't know," we say. "In our own little community we've been really successful and we have a big reputation. We are strong, rich, well-fed, and popular in our sphere here, and you're asking us to be meek, poor, hungry, and persecuted. We've always been taught to be self-reliant and depend on ourselves. We've worked hard to get where we are and we think that's the right way to do things."

But our loving friend says to us: "Yes, I told you to work hard and be self-reliant. I told you that because I knew that I could make your self strong enough to rely upon, and I wanted you to find that out. But, does it surprise you to know that I am the one who made it possible for you to be self-reliant? I provided the resources, the jobs, the environment. I own the company that gave you your opportunities, and I kept my eye on you from the executive suite.

"Everything good came from me. Your utter dependence on me is not new. It has been always true. I have made everything possible and I ask you now, to give it to me. You can trust that I will replace it tenfold if you are willing to lay it down. You can move into the community of mansions and not only receive the good tenfold but also have all the bad removed. Trust me. Take the charity. It will be okay. I promise. And when it is all over, you will be *permanently* strong, rich, well-fed, and popular. But I cannot make you that way until you are willing to feel poor because charity is the only route to the mansion."

"But . . . but . . . if we owe charity for everything, then we feel like we are nothing."

"Ah, now you're coming closer. Keep that thought. If you are nothing in yourself, then how do you feel about the something you're becoming?"

It took a moment before we understood the magnitude of the admission.

After the flood of humility, came the clean feeling of gratitude. We fell on our knees. He could have everything. Everything we had. Everything anyone owed us. Everything. In our unworthiness we were willing to give up even the mansion itself. Our acknowledgment of our huge debt to him left room only for gratitude, not for demands. Gradually, the gratitude began to be accompanied by a peaceful confidence.

As our gratitude expanded even more, we felt a slow but powerful enfolding in the arms of his love. "Come," he said. "Your mansion is prepared."

The kingdoms of glory are debt-free communities. We go there being owed nothing and owing nothing except for the infinite, endless, and humble debt we owe to the Savior, whose charity made that debt-free glory available to us. The debt of restitution both for us and to us will be (and must be) charitably fulfilled—we either accept that charity or we don't move into those kingdoms of glory. We must give the Lord everything we do have and can have. In the end, "after all we can do" (2 Nephi 25:23), we must move into the Lord's communities feeling that we are nothing *without* his charity. For our own good, the Lord makes that a requirement—a requirement of abject humility, of sincere and heartfelt works—but we must be so careful to avoid the illusion that those works will be what moves us into one of those wonderful debt-free communities. So many of us are so proud. If we've incurred a debt, we like to think we can pay it ourselves. If we are owed a debt we want to collect it from the person we think owes us. We dislike the notion that we need help. But we do need help. All of us need it. None of us is capable of moving into those communities without it. We need to value charity above all things instead of being offended by it because it is gratitude for that charity that enables us to accept it and have all the debts paid for us and to us. Charity is beautiful. Charity is our only possible source of perfect love. And yet . . .

Charity in our society has become something scorned. Even our governments work to obliterate it. Entitlements, instead of the temporary helping hand, rule the day. They allow us an illusion of self-reliance. Real self-reliance takes place against a backdrop of the gift and power of God and with an acknowledgment of that base dependence. It is a God-encouraged virtue. But the illusion of *independent* self-reliance (like all illusions) is damning. It is damning because our mind-set is that charity brings a stigma. In the eternal sense, at least, it actually removes all stigmas. In our mind-set, we are less if we accept charity. In the eternal sense, we are "nothing" without it.[7] We turn away from charity with pride, and as a result, turn away from restitution and from peace. The Lord invites us to accept both with humility. *We must change our mind-set about charity from prideful to grateful because gratitude is fundamental.*

⁓

Another kind of ingratitude stems from treasuring up a disadvantaged state—of not wanting to be without our victims' status.

"Then I would impress upon your heart, my daughter, that you should pay close attention to the way God tends to the welfare of the people here in the valley. Little rain falls, but He has given you water from the mountains, and the dew refreshes the meadows and fields each night. Thank God for the good gifts He has given you and don't complain if you think you are lacking something else that you think would be beneficial. You have beautiful golden hair, so do not fret because it isn't curly. Haven't you heard about the woman who sat and wept because she had only a little scrap of pork to give her seven hungry children for Christmas dinner? St. Olav came riding past at that very moment. Then he stretched out his hand over the meat and prayed to God to feed the poor urchins. But when the woman saw that a slaughtered pig lay on the table, she began to cry because she didn't have enough bowls and pots."[8]

This all too common character deficiency (which finds its way into the hearts of all of us from time to time) has its root in some basic tendencies of human nature. First, it seems we are often looking for a 'free lunch.' We are at liberty to seek blessings, but all blessings come with what might be called a price attached (D&C 132:5). We must abide the law of every blessing we desire to receive. We have a role to play. We may be given a slaughtered pig, but we must improvise somehow for bowls and pots in which to put it. Sufficient gratitude for the meat is necessary before we can consider it a blessing instead of a curse to bustle for vessels to put it in—because bustle we must. Even miraculous meat is not a free lunch. We mustn't expect it to be. Our accountant often reminds me that the ability to earn money is not a free lunch, either; nevertheless, we must have sufficient gratitude for our income before we can consider it a blessing to have taxes to pay. We must have sufficient delight in planning a shopping trip before we can stop complaining about paying the price of traffic downtown and the length of time it takes to find a parking place.

On a gospel level, we must love the Lord enough and be grateful enough for his sacrifice, that we consider it a blessing to serve him. We must not find his requirements to be grounds for complaint. We must regard obedience to his law as a bargain at any price if we are to pay it gladly and gratefully. Because even obedience itself brings new blessings (Mosiah 2:24), and never will we remove our need for charity. We must deeply desire to express our gratitude and serve him forever if we are to have the Lord go with us to the judges.

Interestingly, the treasuring up of our disadvantaged status develops because we tend to focus on what we *don't* have. As a child, whenever I or my brothers and sisters were faced with a large blessing and still complained about what it *wasn't*, my mother would say: "Well, I guess it's 'thanks for the *next*, I'm *sure* of *this*.'" It brought us into the focus of being grateful for what we had quickly taken for granted and stopped us from looking covetously to what we didn't yet have. I often repeat this little saying to myself even now when I am tempted to complain. It reminds me that to focus on what I don't have is nothing short of ingratitude for what I have been given. As King Benjamin pointed out, "condemnation is just" for coveting that which we have not received (Mosiah 4:25). Perhaps one reason the tenth commandment "thou shalt not covet" is included in the decalogue is to address the significant sin of ingratitude. Once this particular type of ingratitude—this coveting of what we don't have, this bottomless self-pity—seizes our soul, it is acutely addictive. It really does become a matter of treasuring up our victims' rights. Every one of us, after all, is in some way a victim. If we focus on what we do not have, and therefore on how much more advantaged others are, it seems to make excuse for us to give less. We have so little, after all.

If we indulge in *self*-pity, we unconsciously solicit the pity of others, and if they pity us they won't call on us to do as much and won't think ill of us for what we haven't done. Being pitiable is such a good excuse. And if we are trying to avail ourselves of that excuse, we will seldom find the meekness to go to our Father in Heaven with the true contrition and broken hearts that are necessary for receipt of the charity of the Lord Jesus Christ. We must feel our need for the Savior. Anything that stands in the way of contrition and a broken heart will ultimately stop us from the intense gratitude that is necessary to gain access to the Lord's sweet and generous atonement.

There is also a modern barrier to being grateful enough to accept the Lord's sacrifice as payment. It is the barrier that comes when we declare ourselves to be "not responsible" for our own sins. It is fashionable in today's world to find ourselves guiltless if our behavior can be blamed on some chromosomal combination, or perhaps an emotional handicap of some kind. If our circumstances are less than privileged, that too is considered to render us blameless.

It's certainly entirely possible—even likely—that in many instances the Lord will indeed declare selected individuals "not responsible" for some unrighteous behaviors. It may even be a matter of restitution and restoration of damage that has been done to them. Nevertheless, *we* do not have the right to assign or excuse responsibility. It is imperative that we leave the pronouncement of responsibility (or lack of it) to the Lord. Each person must, in this life, seek charity for their sins and not excuse for them.

"My parents did not give me a proper role model" is damning. A statement such as, "I suffer the guilt of my own bad choices and need the Lord's charity to pay my debt of restitution to those whom I have hurt" can be exalting.

"I never had advantages in life, and so I couldn't be expected to care about others" is damning. Saying instead, "I have been dishonest to others and have taken advantage of them. I will try my whole life to make restitution, but I am so inadequate. I desperately need the Savior's atonement" can be exalting.

Thinking that we are not responsible and therefore excused effectively removes our ability to feel the need for the sacrifice of the Savior. Such thoughts will eliminate any chance for enough gratitude to accept his atonement and thereby access the joy of redemption in our lives. That chance to be so grateful is all-important.

Acceptance of responsibility can be a staggering weight. The Savior knows and understands how heavy it is.

"Come unto me, all ye that labor and are heavy laden, and I will give you rest" (Matthew 11:28).

Declaring ourselves "not responsible" will only stand in the way of us gratefully laying the burden at the Savior's feet. Guilt must be acknowledged before guilt can be washed away.

Probably Alma gives the best description of this process to his son Helaman:

As I was thus racked with torment, while I was harrowed up by the memory of my many sins, behold, I remembered also to have heard my father prophesy unto the people concerning the coming of one Jesus Christ, a Son of God, to atone for the sins of the world. Now, as my mind caught hold upon this thought, I cried within my heart: O Jesus, thou son of God, have mercy on me, who am in the gall of bitterness, and am encircled about by the everlasting chains of death. And now, behold, when I thought this, I could remember my pains no more; yea, I was harrowed up by the memory of my sins no more. And oh, what joy, and what marvelous light I did behold; yea, my soul was filled with joy as exceeding as was my pain! Yea, I say unto you, my son, that there could be nothing so exquisite and so bitter as were my pains. Yea, and again I say unto you, my son, that on the other hand, there can be nothing so exquisite and sweet as was my joy. (Alma 36:17–21)

The joy that Alma describes is the pearl of great price[9] that we should sell everything else to receive. That exquisite joy is what we all seek, but we often cling to self-pity instead. How sad.

It's all right for us to be the striving but imperfect creatures that we are. God knew that we would make mistakes and he provided a way back to his presence. It will be damning, however, if we indulge in the barriers that keep us from finding that straight and narrow way back to him.

Impatience, unbelief, refusal to accept charity, or to sacrifice what we must, a preference for self-pity or a rationalized self-justification—any of these are causes and indications of ingratitude for the Atonement. And all of us are guilty of indulging in these things at one time or another to some degree or another. Still, we must all strive diligently to overcome these flaws in our character. Gratitude is fundamental in developing the patience by which we can possess our souls—the patience to have real hope, hope for restitution because we trust in both justice and mercy.

Notes

1. Stephen E. Robinson, *Believing Christ* (Salt Lake City: Deseret Book, 1992), 9.

2. 2 Peter 1:4.

3. Luke 15.

4. *Hamlet* 3.3.97.

5. "The Rape of Lucrece," in *Shakespeare: The Complete Works,* ed. G. B. Harrison (New York: Harcourt, Brace, & World, 1952), 1564.

6. Mark 9:24.

7. Mosiah 4:11.

8. Sigrid Undset, *Kristin Lavransdatter,* trans. Tina Nunnally (New York: Penguin Books, 1999), 73.

9. Matthew 11:46.

~ 10 ~

ACCEPTING THE ATONEMENT AND RELEASING OUR GUILT

When we forgive others, even though we have total assurance that restitution will be made, it requires our participation in a merciful way. It is an act of love to give that mercy—to accept the restitution. It is a willingness to give up vengeance and hatred. We are asking for the Savior's gift of restitution for those victims' rights that our victimizers cannot pay. Forgiving those who trespass against *us*, means wanting the Lord to make the payment for those who owe us the debt. It is relinquishing the hatred of wanting to settle the score personally with the victimizer. Even though Christ is able to restore us beyond our loss, a hardened heart can be more concerned with the victimizer making the payment than with getting damages settled. Even to accept the premium restitution that the Lord will provide requires a degree of mercy.

When we accept the Lord's charity for ourselves, however—for the wrongs that we have done others and for the damage we have done to our own progression—our participation in the process consists of begging for mercy—not giving it. There is a big difference. It is a difference in degree of abasement—of abject humility. Yes, the hardened heart must be abandoned in both instances, but it is nowhere nearly as self-abasing to accept payment of a debt that is owed to you as it is to know that there must be public and charitable payment of your own debts to others. Gripping as self-pity is, it is not so profound as guilt. It is much less uncomfortable to have others know that you were hurt than it is to have others know that you are responsible for someone else being hurt. I have had the experience of calling my insurance company when I was rear-ended by another car and while I hated the inconvenience there was no embarrassment attached. On the other hand, I have also had to call them to tell the claims representative that I was the one who rear-ended another car. Believe me, it is much worse to be the one at fault.

I'm sure that this difference in intensity of feeling is the reason that people tend to define the Atonement in terms of receiving forgiveness of their own sins and ignore the forgiving of others when they talk about the Atonement. It was guilt that had been washed away for Enos, remember when he felt so weightless. It was guilt that left Alma when he described his joy as exquisite.

When we try to achieve this weightless guiltlessness, this exquisite joy, by trying to "forgive ourselves," it really doesn't work. Believing that it is an act of giving mercy to ourselves instead of an act of begging for mercy, we will *never* achieve the guiltless state because the very fact of believing that it is possible to do it ourselves will be a barrier to receiving it in the way that *is* possible.

I hear, over and over again, "She just can't forgive herself," or "If only he could forgive himself." If only he could, indeed. But he can't. Only Christ can do that. We owe restitution. And we cannot pay that debt to those we have hurt—including ourselves. We can only accept the charity of our Savior who will pay those debts for us, who will leave us debt-free, guilt-free, and in a state of exquisite joy. That's what being forgiven means. Our society tells us that we, ourselves, must pronounce those debts as paid.

We can't do that and the pressure builds into a barrier that will forever stop us from seeing that we don't *have* to do that. If we can't see that it is the Lord who is our Redeemer, we will not be grateful enough to access the glorious rest that he has, as his very purpose, a mind to give us.

Nowhere does the Lord tell us to forgive ourselves. Nowhere does he report that someone did do that. We do not read, for example, that Enos finally reached a point where he could forgive himself. It was the Lord who forgave. And Enos was overwhelmed when the guilt was washed away.

Alma was delivered from his painful guilt only as part of a powerful plea for mercy. As a result, he testified that he was "born of God." He did not say that as a result he was able to convince himself that everything was okay. He knew that he was forgiven, not excused. That was his great joy. People who try in vain to forgive themselves are usually trying to excuse themselves. It doesn't work.

One of the missionaries who served with us when my husband was a mission president had a powerful experience with repentance after he left the mission field. It was not easy. It required many months—what seemed like endless months—of praying and scripture study and service to others. The guilt lingered and lingered. He was in agony. No effort was made to discount the sin, to excuse himself, or to forgive himself. The effort instead was made in a mighty plea for mercy. He reported that after many months of this begging, after many months of acknowledging the absolute power and great goodness of God, he looked in the mirror one day and it was gone. The pain was gone. It was replaced by a joy that was as exquisite as was his pain. He felt the arms of love. He felt the utter charity of the Savior. He was incredulous! "It was just like Alma," he said to us later. "It was just like Alma! It was wonderful!"

I do know that this sudden and strong revelation is not usual. The experience our missionary had at the mirror and that Alma had when he was lifted out of his pit of despair will be elusive to most.

Many of us will recognize the arms of love only after we have been enfolded by them for a good long time. The effort and humility may cause many to experience the "mighty change" behaviorally without a consciousness of it. They may awaken one day to realize, with a quiet surprise, that they have developed a happy confidence from virtue garnishing their thoughts unceasingly. For some, barriers are in place that cause them to resist the mighty change. There are those who focus a bit too much on their own inadequacy instead of on God's omnipotence. This focus problem gives many a reluctance to release the guilt.

Whether the problem is recognition of the Lord's forgiveness or reluctance to accept it, the solution is *not* to unilaterally declare that the guilt is released. The solution is to realign the focus on God's great love and power. We must, with gratitude, remove the barriers to that focus change, so that the love and power of God can be felt. Perhaps it is just that we have a faulty definition of humility. Humility is not a negative self-focus. It is an acknowledged dependence on our Father in Heaven, an understanding that without him, or in comparison to him, we are nothing. A willingness to do whatever he asks of us. When this sort of humility is understood (and indeed internalized) the Lord is able to communicate his love to us and we will feel of his power.

I have always loved the story that Elder Henry B. Eyring tells of helping a young man to recognize how the Lord's love was manifesting in his life and what joy he was already receiving from his benevolent Father in Heaven.

> Once, as a bishop of a ward, I worked with a young man
> who had made great mistakes, but he had been moved by faith

in the Lord Jesus Christ to make long and painful repentance. We were down to the weeks before he was to be married in the temple. I had long before forgiven him in the name of the Church and had given him his temple recommend. But he remembered that I had said, "The Lord will forgive you in his own time and in his own way," and now he was deeply concerned. He came to my office and said: "You told me that the Lord would someday let me know that I was forgiven. But I am going to the temple to marry a wonderful girl. I want to be the best I can be for her. I need to know that I am forgiven. And I need to know now. Tell me how to find out." I said I would try.

He gave me a deadline. As I recall, it was less than two weeks away. Fortunately, during that period of time I went to Salt Lake City and found myself seeing Elder Spencer W. Kimball, then a member of the Quorum of the Twelve, at a social function. It was crowded, and yet he somehow found me. He walked up to me in that crowd and said, "Hal, I understand that you are now a bishop. Do you have anything you would like to ask me?"

I said that I did, but I didn't think that was the place to talk about it. He thought it was. It was an outdoor party. My memory is that we went behind a shrub and there had our interview. Without breaking confidences, I outlined the concerns and the question of this young man in my ward. Then I asked Elder Kimball, "How can he get that revelation? How can he know whether his sins are remitted?"

I thought Elder Kimball would talk to me about fasting or prayer or listening for the still small voice. But he surprised me. Instead he said, "Tell me something about the young man."

I said, "What would you like to know?"

And then he began a series of the most simple questions. Some of the ones I remember were:

"Does he come to his priesthood meetings?"

I said, after a moment of thought, "Yes."

"Does he come early?"

"Yes."

"Does he sit toward the front?"

I thought for a moment and then realized, to my amazement, that he did.

"Does he home teach?"

"Yes."

"Does he go early in the month?"

"Yes, he does."

"Does he go more than once?"

"Yes."

I can't remember the other questions. But they were all like that—little things, simple acts of obedience, of submission. And for each question I was surprised that my answer was always yes. Yes, he wasn't just at all his meetings: he was early; he was smiling; he was there not only with his whole heart, but with the broken heart of a little child, as he was every time the Lord asked anything of him. And after I had said yes to each of his questions, Elder Kimball looked at me, paused, and then very quietly said, "There is your revelation."

Elder Eyring pointed out that the young man was showing the evidence of his mighty change of heart. And then he said something further that still touches me now as tenderly as it did when I first read it:

"My guess is that he has retained a remission of his sins. I don't know if he knew then or if he knows now with the certainty he wanted, but *I am sure of something. When that change of heart comes to me and to you, when we are cleansed and blameless before God, it will be because we have been made pure by the blood of Christ. . . . I must have exercised faith in the Savior long enough and carefully enough* that his grace will be sufficient for me. And I know at least one way to know that is happening in my life—or in yours. You will have put yourself so often in the Master's service, bringing the cleansing companionship of the Holy Ghost, that you will be on the front row, early, whenever and wherever the Master calls. It will be gradual enough that you may not notice. . . . But those with spiritual discernment who love you will know. And the Savior and our Heavenly Father will know. And that is enough."[1]

There are many things we can do for ourselves, but giving ourselves a remission of sins is not one of them. As Elder Eyring said, "It will be because we have been made pure by the blood of Christ." That will always be true.

We seek relief from the Savior and we do not know when or how the relief will come. We mustn't give up to impatience. We do not know what he will require of us and we mustn't weary in well-doing. We must be willing to recognize his love and power when it is manifest in our lives. The time will come when he who knows our hearts, will indeed give us pardon and full restitution. He will encircle us in the arms of his love.

The key is not to say or think: I forgive myself. The key is to say and think: Now that I have done everything possible to change and to make an honest effort at restitution to the persons I have wronged, I need to accept that Christ will do what I cannot. He will pay true and full restitution to them. He will make up the difference. I don't need to forgive myself. I need to gratefully accept the Atonement as the Atonement was intended. I need to understand that the reason the Atonement can remove my guilt is that Christ will pay restitution to my victims. It isn't that Christ will compensate me for my sin. It is that he will compensate my victims to whom I have a debt to restore.

The payment of our debts to our victims and the receipt of the restitution that is due to us should cause us to sing the song of redeeming love. Forgiveness is not something we can give to ourselves, but we can, with hope and surety, work toward receiving it as a divine gift.

Note

1. Henry B. Eyring, *To Draw Closer to God* (Salt Lake City: Deseret Book, 1997), 55–58; emphasis added.

~ 11 ~

HOPE VS. CONDEMNATION

We had eaten lunch with friends in an Asian restaurant. The not-quite-empty platters had been removed from our table, and we'd already laughed over our fortune cookies. "Tell us what you're reading about these days."

I almost wished he hadn't asked. "Same thing I've been reading about for the past few years. It's the Atonement and forgiveness." My voice was much softer than usual. Uncharacteristically, I wanted to let it drop.

These dear friends have burdens of tragedy beyond any that I have even feared having to deal with in my life. They have suffered and are suffering much because of the errors of others. One of their daughters requires total care because of someone else's mistake at the wheel of a car. Their life's journey is uphill constantly—trying to climb and conquer the obstacles that others have put in the way of their earthly peace. I was reluctant. But they prodded me on. "Tell us. Tell us what you're learning."

"Just more about what I already know. It's like all of life's struggles. We can forgive when we value the Atonement enough." Silence followed for a moment while I tried to deal with feeling so awkward. What I had said was true and I knew it, but I didn't say it as if I did because I felt self-righteous, and somehow it sounded

91

platitudinous coming from me to them. "Boy," I said, "listen to me. I sound like Job's friends. Just call me Eliphaz Rasband." (Indeed, it was Eliphaz who accusingly said to Job, "Are the consolations of God small to thee?"[1]) I was uncomfortable with seeing my mirrored image in those who tormented poor Job, and the discomfort was enough to silence me.

If I was worried about of my friends' response, I needn't have been. I had only reminded them of what they already knew as well as I knew, and their humility governed their reaction. The husband got a faraway look in his eye and he said, "Aye, there's the rub." Then he asked sincerely, "How do you get to the point where you value the Atonement that much?"

In the April 2002 general conference Elder Dallin H. Oaks talked about a less-than-contributory member of the Church who once asked him, "What's He [Christ] done for me?" Elder Oaks grieved over that man—his very heart being deeply offended by the question itself.[2]

But there was no such question coming from our dear friends. There was no blasphemous denial of the gift. They were Saints whose souls had been stirred by the spirit, and they felt to love the Lord. They knew that the Atonement was a great gift, and they were striving to live worthily to receive its blessings. Nevertheless, they struggled to value the Atonement *enough*. Theirs is the same anguish that was felt by the good sister mentioned in chapter four, the sister who outlined for us the types of challenges that make forgiving hard. These friends suffered the same anxiety that is felt by so many—many who do not even have such weighty mistreatment to forgive. "How do you get to the point where you value the Atonement that much?"

That question haunts the mind of every good Christian who wants to forgive but still finds it a struggle. The struggle may well be because we lack understanding of what the Atonement does.

The law of Moses was designed to fill that gap in our knowledge—to teach us what the Atonement does and to teach us that the Atonement redeems us from the Fall and makes restitution available.

Our friends at lunch that day certainly know the problem of forgiveness and desire to solve it, but the fundamentals of how to work it out are missing. The question of how to value the Atonement enough comes, not so much out of an unwillingness to work at the problem of forgiveness, but rather a need for the drill. The master teacher who taught me mathematics at the blackboard in his basement left me with a great respect for the value of the drill. When we learn the concepts thoroughly, problems tend to be solved much more readily.

We are children of Israel. Paul said that the law of Moses was a schoolmaster to bring the children of Israel to Christ. And how to get to Christ is the real question here. Understanding the different kinds of sacrifice and the symbols of proxy atonement are important, but there is more that we must understand. In accepting what I came to call the Old Testament Drill and its ground rules, we can find some of the answers to the questions as to what the Atonement actually does—and therefore why and how we can come to value it so completely.

As I thrashed about with our friends' question in the weeks that followed our lunch together, I realized that I had given them an illumination of a problem that was already brightly paraded before their spiritual faces. The hope that comes from knowing how to work the problem is in the drill. The danger that all of us face when we teach the doctrine of forgiveness, or any other doctrine for that matter, is that we dwell on the problem (we preach) instead of helping find the way to solve it (by teaching). My friends, that day, brought me back to the matter of solution, back really to hope. The danger in our initial conversation (when

I sounded so similar indeed to Eliphaz) was that my answer was much closer to preaching than it was to the teaching they were asking for.

The law of Moses—the drill from the Master Teacher—avoids that danger. It teaches without preaching. It is such a lesson in fundamentals that it gives hope instead of condemnation. As one author describes it:

"God as the sovereign Lord and Creator gives His law to man as an act of sovereign grace."[3]

The law of Moses is a true and gentle path toward understanding the blessing of the atonement of Christ.

The law of Moses drills us on the requirements of the law and the demands of justice. With the details of what justice means, it gives solid understanding of the jots and tittles that the Lord fulfilled with the Atonement. The law of Moses doesn't preach to us, it teaches us, while at the same time reassuring us that the master we love enough will go with us to the judges and see that all the requirements of both justice and mercy are met. Had the Lord simply preached a sermon to the ancient Israelites, it would have condemned them, they having already expressed their fright at what seemed to them to be more than they could do. Instead he gave them a long-term, slow and steady opportunity to understand what the plan of salvation does for us. It was the perfect example of teaching: It made available understanding, both of what was necessary and how the necessity could be reached. Justice is necessary. Mercy is how it can be reached. Love for our families and our master is how both can be accessed. All real teaching must follow this model—the model of hope instead of condemnation.

I think of our friends with whom we had lunch and discarded our fortune cookies that day. I think of their sorrows and their children's sorrows. And the hope I learned from the drill anchors my soul. Our friends' daughter will walk and talk again. She will have the opportunity to have a husband worthy of her beauty and with him eternal increase can bless her life forever. Our friends' other burdens will also be lifted, and all will be restored double or more—indeed infinitely—just as what Job had lost was restored to him. Restoring is what the Atonement does! They can count on that restoration. They may not know the hour or the day, but they can "with patience wait for it."[4] They have brought their burden to the Lord, and he will give them rest.

There is no greater hope than knowing that we were under the law and that the law of Moses is fulfilled.

Joseph Smith said, "Christ himself fulfilled all righteousness in becoming obedient to the law which he had given to Moses on the mount, and therefore magnified it and made it honorable instead of destroying it."[5]

Notes

1. Job 15:11.

2. Dallin H. Oaks, "The Gospel in Our Lives," *Ensign,* May 2002, 33.

3. Rousas John Rushdoony, *The Institutes of Biblical Law* (Nutley, N.J.: Craig Press, 1973), 8.

4. Romans 8:25.

5. Joseph Smith, *Teachings of the Prophet Joseph Smith,* sel. Joseph Fielding Smith (Salt Lake City: Deseret Book, 1976), 276.

~ 12 ~

IF YOU LOVE 'EM,
CUT 'EM SOME SLACK

As you internalize the drill, you will find a most amazing and delightful consequence in your behavior. You will stop pausing. As you develop faith in and gratitude for the charity of the Savior, you will find yourself showing a kind of smooth and seamless mercy to others. Knowing that you will ultimately have at least equivalent restitution makes the offenses that you suffer not worth worrying about—at least not in any significant way. And the byproduct of that loss of worry, that release of your victim's rights for full payment, will settle on you like "the dews from heaven"—equally refreshing and life-renewing. That good news is what Amulek was describing in Alma 34:31: "If ye will repent and harden not your hearts, immediately shall the great plan of redemption be brought about unto you."

It is that same beloved description of the relief of pressure that we find in Psalm 119:165: "Great peace have they which love thy law: and nothing shall offend them."

To love the law of the Lord includes taking heart from it. It includes making every effort to rid ourselves of the barriers to gratitude that we all—with Satan's help—indulge in. It means beginning to live our lives with a generally forgiving spirit. It means experiencing an artless breadth of understanding for the people in our lives—an empathy that enriches us and calms us. We, after all—thanks to the payment of the Messiah—have nothing to lose from their offenses.

That empathy, that constant companionship of the forgiving spirit—that's called love. It is what the Savior intended for us to feel when he commanded us to love one another. The parable of the good Samaritan makes that clear. For centuries, the Samaritans had been the victims of much hatred and abuse from Jews. Any Samaritan had reason to take offense from any Jew. But empathy overtook the good Samaritan instead, and he firmly took hold of the Golden Rule to give care to this needy Jew—this needy Jew who doubtless would have hated him. The Samaritan did not give hate for hate.

I wonder if the Jews that Christ was talking to when he gave this parable, recognized the allusion from Exodus 23:5: "If thou see the ass of him that hateth thee lying under his burden, and wouldest forbear to help him, thou shalt surely help with him."

For the Samaritan did see the burden of him that hated him, and he did surely help with him. I wonder if they were willing to see that Christ was telling the story of someone they hated who was living the law of Moses. Indeed, as John W. Welch has pointed out, he was actually telling the story of someone who was *fulfilling* the law of Moses.[1]

When we have accepted the charity of him who fulfilled the law of Moses, we begin to become loving in that good Samaritan kind of way. We will, of course, not reach that pinnacle of empathy overnight, perhaps not even in this life, but when we find ourselves taking offense less and less, we know we are on our way.

Sometimes it might be easier to understand how the difference in us can be manifest, by looking at others in our lives. Others whom we love and who love us.

We all have people in our lives who make us feel comfortable and happy. We all have people in our lives in whose presence we feel uncomfortable and stressed. I remember well one day that I paid a visit to a loved one in the latter category. The tension I felt was tangible. I had made every effort to please her but I felt insecure. I felt the eye of judgment, no, lets call it condemnation, on my every move. I felt that my every flaw was on display. Some of them were mentioned, some not, but in any case I felt the inevitability of offending during the entire visit.

Directly following that visit, I stopped at the home of a friend. This friend is in the first category. Being with her makes me feel comfortable and loved. I walked in her door and breathed deeply. I took in the beautiful feelings that came from her love of me. It was not that I now felt flawless. On the contrary I felt much more at ease admitting my shortcomings—both to myself and to her. I knew that she would not take offense at any of them. She was, for me, a hearth where I could warm myself from the cold winds of criticism.

After a while I thanked her for her loving spirit and I asked her a question. "What does it mean to you to love somebody?"

"I don't know," she said. "I just love 'em." I smiled because I should have known that would be her answer.

"Well, I've been thinking," I said. (I was really still just thinking, but doing it out loud. I felt safe enough with my friend to do that.) "I guess, when I love somebody, what that means is that I cut 'em some slack." She looked at me with a puzzled face. "What on earth do you mean by that?"

"Well, I mean, if I love you, you don't have to measure up. If you make a mistake I'm willing to just call it a mistake and not think ill of you for it. I used to laugh at *Love Story*—you know, the business about loving somebody meaning you don't have to say you're sorry, and I still kind of disagree with that because we do need to acknowledge when we've messed up. Loving doesn't excuse a person from manners or consideration. But I think what it really means is that forgiveness is sort of, well, automatic among people who love one another. It's just sort of there as a continuous gift, you know?"

She did know. "Yeah," she said. "It's a beautiful, secure feeling. I'd never really connected it to loving somebody before. But maybe that's one definition of love. Maybe that's how you can tell if somebody really loves you. Kind of like you said: if you love me cut me some slack. Don't make me measure up. People I love, well, if they're being loyal to me, if they're trying to be good to me, if they're not actually trying to hurt me—well if they don't hurt me, I cut 'em some slack."

"Yes, you do," I said. "And it feels so good that your friends want to be more and more loyal to you. I love that you cut me some slack."

"You know" (and now I was thinking out loud again), "I think what some people do is to say, in effect, 'if you love me keep my commandments.' They have their own yardstick you have to live up to in order to get their approval—maybe even their tolerance. Their focus is always on that yardstick and whether or not you're meeting it." My friend broke in: "But God says that, doesn't he? If you love me keep my commandments?"

"Yeah, but that's my point. God *gets* to say that. He's God. But we aren't God. We don't get to put those kinds of requirements on other human beings. And besides, I sort of get the feeling that while God points out the yardstick as the way to show our love, it's *us* he's focused on. Not the yardstick itself. And that's very different from what I'm talking about."

"Well," my friend said after a minute or two, "maybe if its continuous forgiveness that we're talking about, well then what you're saying is that God will forgive whom he will forgive but of us it is required to forgive all men."[2]

"Yes!" It was one of those joyful exclamations that could just as easily have been punctuated by a fist in the air. "We need to provide a climate of continuous forgiveness—not a lowering of our standards but a little bit of slack as we see one another unable to reach them. I guess I'm just feeling the need to plead: If you love me, cut me some slack. It's forgiveness and it's patience."

"Done!" said my friend. "You've got all the slack you need."

"I know," I answered, "and it makes me want to be a better human being. And yes, I do think that's what it means to love and be loved." There was some silence and then my friend said, "Funny, but I always feel that God is cutting me slack, too. His commandments aren't really hurdles to clear for his love, but wheels to ride toward it. Maybe that's why he's the only one that gets to say, 'If you love me keep my commandments.'"

"Exactly!" I felt understood. "When we say 'keep my commandments' to one another, they *are* hurdles we have to clear to get to each other's love, and we're intimidated trying to clear them. But you're so right. God really doesn't set it up that way. It's like the commandments *are* his love, and its okay because he's the all-knowing one and he gives us the wheels to get to him. That's part of the love, eh?"

"Ah, yes," she answered.

We both got contemplative. I can't remember which one of us said: "I guess even the requirement that they be loyal or not hurtful—I guess even those 'commandments' are really only God's to give. I guess we need to cut *everybody* some slack. Even people who hate us. Only God gets to make conditions of loyalty and effort."

"Wow!" We said almost together.

⌒

What is it that makes some people able to overlook our flaws while others focus on every one of them? Why are we so quick to anger because of the faults of others? Why are we so swift in our efforts to perfect the whole human race rather than working on that process in ourselves? Well I think I know why. I think it is because we haven't learned yet that we can love on command and that when we love, we cut people some slack. We think that love is something that just sort of happens as a matter of inclination. We forget that we have been commanded to love and that if we couldn't choose to love we wouldn't have been commanded to do it. I think we haven't allowed ourselves to feel the warmth and comfort of God's love for us and we fail to recognize our responsibility to give that warmth to others. To feel unloved is a paralyzing sensation. The truth of it is that God's love is quintessentially slack-cutting if he knows that we are truly loyal to him, truly trying with our obedience never to hurt him. (He can and does make that a condition.) It's important to acknowledge that God's commandments are messages born of the love he has for us—the love he wants us to fully find access to.

We really can get that comfort directly from the source of all love. The love is there for collection. And we can give it to others. Cutting others some slack is allowing the spirit of forgiveness to enter our constant consciousness. It is a continual remembering of the fact that the atoning sacrifice has been made, that the price has been paid for our sins and for the sins of those who have sinned against us. It is moving smoothly and seamlessly toward keeping the Lord's commandment to love one another. It's living the spirit of forgiveness at all times because we no longer have to consider the cost, knowing in advance, as we do, that it has been paid. All of this grows easier after studying the Old Testament drill of justice and mercy. It is the delightful surprise that begins to come into our lives when the drill is internalized. Mercy understood begins to be mercy given. Undaunted, confident, and optimistic, we stop pausing in our progression.

I was talking recently with the children of some acquaintances that have lately been divorced. Both parents of the young adult children were guilty of infidelity, not to mention several other lapses in acceptable behavior. Their children, however, were not content to call it a two-sided problem. Nor did they both take the same side in the argument. "Mother was cold and unloving," said the daughter. "There's no excuse for being that kind of wife. No wonder Dad went off and did what he did. I admit what he did was wrong, but I can certainly understand all of it. He's a wonderful man."

"But Dad made promises to Mom," the son countered.

"So did Mom, and she broke them."

"But its understandable when she felt rejected! Dad destroyed our home!"

"No he didn't! Mom did that years ago!"

It was not hard to figure out that the daughter loved her father but not her mother and that for the son it was *vice versa*. Simple. The daughter was willing to cut her father some slack but not her mother, and the son cut slack for his mother but not his father. Of course to cut the slack, they were engaging in blame for the one they didn't love. Not unusual.

Listening to them it seemed they felt they had to either accuse or excuse each parent. What a freeing feeling it would have been for them to realize that forgiving doesn't mean playing God, it only means obeying God. It doesn't mean justifying. It means loving. When we acknowledge wrong with the understanding that restitution will come, we can begin to have empathy and we can cut some slack. We can simply and mercifully love. We can extend our hearts, knowing that, in the final day, all damages will be paid, all wrongs set to right.

In our more earnest moments, I'm sure all of us feel sadness that we must admit that we find fault with—and therefore lack love for—others whom we thought we 'loved, but . . .' Nevertheless, we have to face it if we are going to fight it. In a peaceful world, there is no such thing as 'I love him, but . . .' There is only 'I love him.' We must stop imposing on others the obligation to keep *our* commandments. When we learn to love, and we learn to cut some slack because we learn that acknowledging hurt is not accusing, and forgiving is not excusing. We can fight the tendency in ourselves to accuse or excuse by facing the fact that what we are doing is pausing at the blackboard of life. We pause in the middle of trying to work out the problems because we are having difficulty accepting the charity of Christ. We all must nudge ourselves back to the drill and work harder at getting the delightful result of becoming a seamlessly empathetic forgiving climate for the people that God has put into our lives. That is what love is. And that is what we are all trying to learn to do. Love. We can clearly and easily measure our progress or lack of it. If we love 'em, we cut 'em some slack. Mercy will always be important.

Notes

1. John W. Welch, "The Parable of the Good Samaritan," *BYU Studies* 38, no. 2 (1999): 50–115.
2. D&C 64:10.

~ 13 ~

PARENTS AND CHILDREN

A good many years ago some dear friends of ours were bidding farewell to their oldest son as he left for the mission field. My husband and I attended the sacrament meeting and listened tenderly as each member of the family spoke. (This was back in "the olden days," when such things were permissible.) The young man's father stood up and we smiled before he even said a word. We expected his remarks to be a little bit lively. He would be brief, we were sure, but almost certainly entertaining. He was that kind of man.

What followed surprised us. On this occasion he was gentle and subdued. The situation was obviously piercing his soul. It was not a time for witticism.

He thanked his son for the lessons that he had learned in the parenting of such a noble young man. And then he said something that hit me hard. He said: "I hope my son will forgive me for the lessons that I have learned at his expense."

I didn't hear much else of what he said. My mind was filled with the thought of all the lessons that I have learned at the expense of others. Friends, family, teachers, students—but most of all my children because all parents do indeed learn their most expensive lessons at a toll their children must pay. I was moved to tears. I've never forgotten that moment.

I try now, not to forget to ask for that particular kind of forgiveness in every circumstance for which it is appropriate. I am constantly aware of the need for that forgiveness. I am grateful for mercy from everyone who has given it to me, but, like our friend, most of all I'm grateful for it from my children. There is a reason that the desire for forgiveness and the gratitude for it are more acute with one's children. The reason does not have to do with what we want for ourselves but with what we want for those children. We want thorough healing for them.

While all who have forgiven me have added to my well-being by letting me feel their love and mercy, I know that those who have forgiven me have received their own relief as well. By accepting the Lord's atonement as payment for my sins against them, they have received peace.

Above all, parents want the blessing of that relief for their children. It is a longing for their children's joy. All parents know that they have put barriers in the paths of their children's pursuit of peace and each would pray earnestly for the children's ability to remove those barriers with forgiveness through faith in the restitution of the atonement of Jesus Christ.

Parents too, often have much to forgive in their children. Children, after all, by the very nature of the relationship, learn many lessons at the expense of their parents. Many parents harbor hurts that children have inflicted upon them. The pain can be great. The anguished need for forgiveness from parents is universal because every one of us is a child. And every child learns lessons at the expense of his parents. Each of us has much to seek forgiveness of from our mothers and fathers. Restitution through the Atonement is particularly sweet in that quarter.

If ever there were a relationship that required bilateral slack-cutting, a relationship that required constant seamless empathetic mercy, it is the parent-child connection—particularly as the children get older. We parents and children have learned so much at each other's expense. Because we love each other so intensely, we ask for each other's continuous forgiveness. Also because we love each other so intensely, we should give it. With so much history together, it is imperative that we understand that none of us can hurt each other eternally if we bring our heartache and bruises to the Savior. The Savior can and will heal us all. Both parents and children.

I received a particular witness of this truth in a class one day right after a reading of 3 Nephi 17:23, 24. There is no more beautiful section in the scripture.

> And he spake unto the multitude, and said unto them: Behold your little ones. And as they looked to behold they cast their eyes towards heaven, and they saw the heavens open, and they saw angels descending out of heaven as it were in the midst of fire; and they came down and encircled those little ones about, and they were encircled about with fire; and the angels did minister unto them.

The very language is always enough to bring tears to my eyes. But this time there was something to come that was even more touching for me.

It was a beautiful Sabbath morning and I was sitting by one of my sons in Sunday School. The teacher asked this question about the blessing of the little ones about which we had just read: "What is really happening here?"

My son answered, with gravity: "I think the children are being healed from the sins of the fathers."

He was, perhaps, thinking of his own role as a parent, as well as his role as a child. I know I was thinking of my role as a parent at first. Then I thought for a moment too, of my role as a child. I knew instantly that someday, if I can be as a little child, the angels will minister unto me. And I will be healed from the sins of generations of fathers.

All who have blundered and all who have known and acted upon malice in their hearts need the ministering of the angels for those whom they have hurt. The thought of having that healing come to the people we have damaged is astounding in its comfort. It is a joy and a relief of guilt that is beyond comprehension. That splendid release of guilt always reminds me of Enos, who was so amazed at the glorious relief when his guilt was washed away. Christ can save us from the endless agony of having debts out there needing to be paid; debts that we are totally incapable of paying—even though making the effort becomes our dedicated priority as part of our repentance process. Alma the Younger, for instance, devoted his entire life to the restitution process. His understanding of the principle must have been keen, his gratitude for it intense.

Or maybe you think of your own need for the ministering of angels. Many, whether they be your parents, your children, or perfect strangers, have blundered—with or without malice—and left you with that need.

The image of the healing of those children will forever be in my consciousness. What a blessing it is to know that we live under the law of restitution, and it will be given our children, and given us.

~ 14 ~

"I WILL FEAR NO EVIL: FOR
THOU ART WITH ME"

If you could go to war—a war that would really end all wars for you—with a guarantee that you could win a sweet victory and that, while you might suffer some flesh wounds, no injury would leave permanent scars, would you go? If you knew that the enemy could temporarily hurt you, but could not take your eternal life or leave you in any way lastingly maimed or troubled, would you fight? Of course you would. Of course you have. That was the plan of our Father in Heaven for all of us.

We are all in the presence of our enemies, but Christ has prepared our ultimate table. And so we take his rod and his staff, and we fear no evil. The absence of that fear is the blessing that Amulek talked about when he said, "immediately shall the great plan of redemption be brought about unto you" (Alma 34:31).

It's true that full restitution itself may not be immediate, but the great peace that descends when the spirit finally witnesses that the healing will come—that *is* immediate. The peace comes with a flood of love and is accompanied by a thrill of surety in our hope. Then comes the deep and dedicated patience of the truly converted. Because, as Isaiah said, "But they that wait upon the Lord shall renew their strength" (Isaiah 40:31).

No enemy has been given the power to choose whether we

will achieve that strong, sure spiritual life. Only we have that power—the power of faith in the Lord Jesus Christ.

Even a hopeful attraction to belief can lead to faith. Alma called it desire and said we can begin with only that (Alma 32:27). If we experiment upon the word and don't cast the desire out with our unbelief, we can feel the seed of faith and truth swelling in our breasts.

"And because of your diligence and your faith and your patience with the word in nourishing it, that it may take root in you, behold, by and by ye shall pluck the fruit thereof, which is most precious, which is sweet above all that is sweet, and which is white above all that is white, yea, and pure above all that is pure; and ye shall feast upon this fruit even until ye are filled, that ye hunger not, neither shall ye thirst" (Alma 32:42).

Alma is describing the realization of the Lord's love, for us and for others. That is the exquisite joy that he experienced as a young man when his sins were forgiven him. That is the fruit of the Tree of Life—indeed the fruit that we came to earth to partake of.[1] That is the pearl of great price that the Savior promised. That is hope that is sure, and patience that is profound. That is walking in green pastures beside the still waters. That is receiving both justice and mercy. And that's what forgiving means.

In the words of Elder Jeffrey Holland:

"With his mighty arm around us and lifting us, we face life more joyfully even as we face death more triumphantly. Only on the strong shoulders of the Master can we 'fear not.' Only in his embrace is there safety."[2]

The plan of the Father is thrillingly and magnificently conceived. Jehovah gave the children of Israel an instructive drill of the immutable law, and then—with generosity and love beyond our comprehension—he fulfilled every jot and tittle of it himself.

"For he hath answered the ends of the law, and he claimeth all